SEAFIRE
VS
A6M ZERO-SEN

The Pacific 1945

DONALD NIJBOER

First published in Great Britain in 2009 by Osprey Publishing,
Midland House, West Way, Botley, Oxford OX2 0PH, UK
443 Park Avenue South, New York, NY 10016, USA
E-mail: info@ospreypublishing.com

A CIP catalogue record for this book is available from the British Library

Print ISBN: 978 1 84603 433 6
PDF e-book ISBN: 978 1 84603 875 4

Edited by Tony Holmes
Cockpit, gunsight, three-view and armament scrap view artwork by Jim Laurier
Cover artwork by Gareth Hector and Wiek Luijken
Battlescene by Wiek Luijken
Page layout by Ken Vail Graphic Design, Cambridge, UK
Index by Margaret Vaudrey
Typeset in ITC Conduit and Adobe Garamond
Maps by Bounford.com
Originated by PDQ Digital Media Solutions, Suffolk, UK
Printed in China through Bookbuilders

09 10 11 12 13   10 9 8 7 6 5 4 3 2 1

FOR A CATALOGUE OF ALL BOOKS PUBLISHED BY OSPREY MILITARY AND
AVIATION PLEASE CONTACT:

North America
Osprey Direct, c/o Random House Distribution Center, 400 Hahn Road, Westminster, MD
21157
E-mail: uscustomerservice@ospreypublishing.com

ALL OTHER REGIONS
Osprey Direct, The Book Service Ltd, Distribution Centre, Colchester Road, Frating Green,
Colchester, Essex, CO7 7DW, UK
E-mail: customerservice@ospreypublishing.com

www.ospreypublishing.com

Osprey Publishing is supporting the Woodland Trust, the UK's leading woodland
conservation charity, by funding the dedication of trees.

Seafire cover art

Who shot down Sub Lt Freddie Hockley of 887 Naval
Air Squadron (NAS)? On the morning of 15 August
1945, Sub Lt Hockley was leading five Seafire IIIs as
close and middle cover for six Avengers over Odaki Bay,
near Tokyo. Twelve A6M Zero-sens approached the
formation from above and astern and began their attack.
Sufficient time was available for the Seafires to counter
the bounce, but owing to R/T failure, Hockley failed to
see the danger and was shot down. It is not clear as to
which Japanese unit was responsible. Two groups were
active that morning – Zero-sens and J2M Raidens from
the 302nd Kokutai and Zero-sens from the 252nd
Kokutai. (*Cover artwork by Wiek Luijken*)

A6M Zero-sen cover art

At 0725 hrs on 1 April 1945, Sub Lt R. H. Reynolds of
894 NAS engaged his first kamikaze after pursuing
the Zero-sen through the British fleet's Gun Defence
Zone. The Seafire pilot opened fire on the A6M5 at
long range and with extreme deflection. Nevertheless,
Reynolds scored cannon strikes on the port wing root of
the Japanese naval fighter. Before he could attain a better
shooting angle, however, the Zero-sen rolled and dove
straight into the aircraft carrier HMS *Indefatigable*.
(*Cover artwork by Gareth Hector*)

Title page photo

With the war now over, the British Pacific Fleet was
quickly reduced in strength. Even with its poor deck
handling and landing performance, the Seafire continued
to soldier on with No 24 Naval Fighter Wing, seen here
aboard HMS *Indefatigable* in September 1945. The wing
then went ashore at RN Air Station Schofields in
Australia from 18 September to 22 November 1945.
(*Fleet Air Arm Museum*)

CONTENTS

INTRODUCTION

The Spitfire/Seafire and the A6M Zero-sen are two of the most recognisable and iconic fighters of World War II. While one has come to represent a symbol of freedom, the Zero-sen has been cast as the aggressor. In terms of form and function, they are arguably two of the most elegant and beautiful fighters ever built.

Designed and constructed for very different purposes, the Spitfire/Seafire and A6M Zero-sen should have never met in combat. While the Spitfire was 'adapted' to fulfil a role for which it was never intended, the A6M Zero-sen was purpose built from the ground up as a naval fighter, and it proved to be one of the finest aircraft of its type to see action in World War II. And when both met for the final air combats of this global conflict, their roles had ironically been reversed. Seafire IIIs were flying from carrier decks while late mark A6M Zero-sens were being used as ground-based interceptors and suicide bombers. Tasked with carrying out very different roles for which they were designed, only one would be victorious.

The Seafire emerged from an urgent requirement by the Fleet Air Arm for a fast single-engined fighter (it did not possess such an aircraft at the beginning of the war) capable of meeting land-based opponents on better or equal terms. After proving itself during the Battle of Britain, the Spitfire was soon being closely scrutinised by the Admiralty, who quickly demanded a navalised version for its carriers. A Spitfire V was duly fitted with an arrestor hook and slinging points, and during Christmas week 1941, deck suitability trials were conducted aboard HMS *Illustrious*. Further carrier trials took place during March–April 1942, and they proved completely successful.

Meanwhile, in the Pacific, A6M2 Zero-Sens were flying circles around a mixed force of British, Dutch, Australian and American fighters. The Allies were waging a battle for survival, as their P-36s, P-39s, P-40s, Hurricanes and Buffalos were proving to be little more than cannon fodder for the Imperial Japanese Navy's Zero-sen units.

The psychological impact of the A6M2's initial success on Allied pilots was profound. It raised the bar, and soon all British and American fighters were being judged by the standards it set. But as the war progressed, and the Allies forced the Japanese onto the defensive, it fell upon the Zero-sen to defend the empire.

When the Seafire III entered the Pacific war, the Imperial Japanese Navy Air Force (IJNAF) was a mere shadow of its former self – it was critically short of fuel, pilots and quality aircraft. The once vaunted Zero-sen was forced to soldier on, and while new versions had been produced, it remained completely outclassed by the latest crop of Allied fighters such as the P-38, Corsair, Hellcat, P-47, P-51 and Seafire.

By mid 1944, the fate of Japan was all but sealed. In the race towards the Philippines, US Army Air Force and carrier-based US Navy squadrons had all but decimated whole units of the Japanese Army Air Force (JAAF) and IJNAF. What bases they had not destroyed they simply bypassed in one of the most effective tactics of the war. Whole units were left to rot and starve where they stood.

In order to support the United States' final offensive push towards the Japanese home islands, a formidable British carrier fleet was proposed. On 22 November 1944, Adm Sir Bruce Fraser hoisted his flag as commander-in-chief of the newly formed British Pacific Fleet (BPF). Aboard the carriers, No 24 Naval Fighter Wing (joined in March 1945 by No 38 Naval Fighter Wing) was equipped with Seafire F IIIs and L IIIs. Their assigned task was a formidable one. The 40 Seafires of 887 and 894 Naval Air Squadrons (NAS) were to provide the bulk of the fleet fighter defence – they made up just 27 percent of the total BPF fighter strength. The rest of the fighters, namely 12 Fireflies, 38 Hellcats and 73 Corsairs, would be used in the escort and fighter sweep roles.

The Seafire F III and L III would prove to be two of the best medium and low-level fighters of the war. In 1945, they were still the fastest and steepest climbing Allied interceptors. Even against the latest marks of the Zero-sen – the A6M5c – the Seafire had a considerable edge in level speed, rate of climb and diving speed. If it could not always force an opponent to fight, it could at least break off combat at will and return to fight another day. Developed from the Spitfire, the Seafire was a remarkable achievement, and its performance as a naval fighter was a lasting tribute to its brilliant design.

This mixed formation is led by a captured Nakajima Ki-84 Hayate, code named 'Frank' – this example was flown by the Technical Air Intelligence Unit based at Clark Field, in the Philippines, in January 1945. Other aircraft in the formation include a P-51D, F6F Hellcat and a Seafire III. While the oldest design in the group, the Seafire was still one of the best medium to low-level fighters of the war. (Australian War Memorial Negative Number AC0180)

CHRONOLOGY

An A6M2 Type 21 is seen lashed to the flightdeck of the IJN carrier *Akagi* whilst it sails in Hitokappu Bay, in the Kurile Islands, in late November 1941. The Japanese fleet gathered here prior to heading south for the surprise attack on Pearl Harbor. (Australian War Memorial Negative Number P03172.002)

1922
December   Japan launches the world's first purpose designed carrier, *Hosho*.

1934
1 December   British Air Ministry issues a contract to Supermarine for the new Rolls-Royce PV 12 Merlin-powered monoplane fighter.

1936
5 March   Prototype Type 300 (later christened Spitfire) makes its first flight from Eastleigh airfield.

1938
August   RAF's No. 19 Sqn at Duxford is first unit equipped with Spitfire I.

1939
1 April   Mitsubishi A6M Zero prototype makes its maiden flight at Kagamigahara airfield.
May   Royal Navy regains control of its aviation arm, the Fleet Air Arm, from the RAF, which had controlled it since 1 April 1918.

1940
19 August   12 Mitsubishi A6M2 Model 11 Zero-sens of the 12th Kokutai perform the type's first combat mission, escorting 54 Mitsubishi G3M2 Type 96 bombers on a raid on the Chinese city of Chungking.

1941
September   The Admiralty obtains permission to procure 'Sea Spitfires', and requests 400 of the latest type – Mk VCs. The Air Ministry offers just 250, of which 48 are Mk VBs and the remaining 202 Mk VCs.
7 December   Imperial Japanese Navy (IJN) carrier aircraft launch attack on US Navy's Pacific Fleet base at Pearl Harbor, Hawaii. 108 Zero-sens provide fighter cover and strafe field installations.

1942
10 January   CO Royal Navy Fighter School, Lt Cdr H. P. Bramwell, makes the first landing of a modified 'Sea' Spitfire VB aboard HMS *Illustrious*, anchored in the River Clyde. The name Seafire is officially adopted.
June   The first Seafire IB (modified version of production Mk VB) is taken on charge by Royal Navy. That same day, first purpose-built Seafire IIC is also delivered. Both versions are powered by Merlin 45 engines. Majority of converted Mk VB airframes used for training purposes.
4–5 June   Battle of Midway. IJN badly

defeated and loses four carriers and ten percent of its fighter pilots. Turning point in the Pacific War.

October The only frontline squadron to be completely equipped with the Seafire IB was 801 NAS, which was embarked in HMS *Furious* from October 1942 to September 1944. 50 Seafire IICs are delivered and four squadrons equipped.

October A5M3 Model 32 enters combat over Solomon Islands. It has squared wing tips and is code named 'Hamp'.

November Operation *Torch* sees the invasion of North Africa. Five Seafire squadrons took part aboard the carriers HMS *Furious, Argus, Formidable* and *Victorious.*

November First folding wing Seafire III flies in the second week of November. The F III is fitted with a Merlin 55 engine and four-bladed propeller. 103 are built. These are followed by the L III version, equipped with the Merlin 55M (1,060 are built).

1943
August A6M5 Model 52 Zero is rushed into production. Speed is 351mph at 19,700ft.

27 November First Seafire F IIIs reach 894 NAS.

1944
15–27 August Operation *Dragon* sees invasion of southern France. Fighter cover and offensive operations by Seafire units 879, 899, 807 and 809 NASs.

September First A6M5c Model 52c Zero-sen is completed. It is the most heavily armed and armoured Zero-sen built, with two 20mm cannons and three 13.2mm machine guns.

25 October First kamikaze attack of the war. Bomb-laden Zero-sens from the 201st Kokutai sink escort carrier USS *St Lo* (CVE-63).

1945
4 January Operation *Lentil* sees Sumatra oil refinery at Pangkalan Brandon attacked. Seafires from 887 and 894 NASs provide Combat Air Patrols (CAP).

March–April Operation *Iceberg* supports invasion of Okinawa. 887 and 894 NASs fly CAPs from HMS *Indefatigable.*

1 April Sub Lt R. H. Reynolds, in a Seafire L III, downs two A6M5s. These are the first Seafire victories against the Zero-sen. He is the only Seafire pilot to make ace in World War II.

4–25 May Operation *Iceberg II* supports Okinawa invasion. 887 and 894 NASs fly CAPs.

July–August Operation *Olympic I* sees strikes on Japanese home islands by Seafires of Nos 24 and 38 Wings, emabarked in *Indefatigable* and *Implacable*, respectively.

15 August Last Fleet Air Arm combats. Seafires from 887 and 894 NASs down seven A6M5s for loss of one of their own.

The folding wings of the Seafire III were not hydraulically powered (unlike their American counterparts), and this photo reveals just how labour intensive this work really was. This Seafire of No 38 Naval Fighter Wing is being made ready for another sortie in June 1945. The weight penalty that came with the folding wing was 125lbs. (Australian War Memorial Negative Number 019032)

DESIGN AND DEVELOPMENT

SEAFIRE

The Seafire was a fighter born out of desperation. When war broke out in September 1939, the Royal Navy's fleet structure had been designed mainly to fight Japan, not Germany. The fear that Japan would seize the riches of its Eastern empire drove Britain to develop aircraft carriers that did not require fighter aircraft. British naval aircraft procurement concentrated on the problems of a decisive fleet battle. During the inter-war period the Royal Navy assumed that if its aircraft could not sink the enemy's capital ships alone, the best they could do was to slow down the enemy fleet and leave it to the battleships to finish them off.

British aircraft carrier design (armoured hangars) and the belief that the vessels' anti-aircraft guns would offer sufficient protection also greatly influenced aircraft procurement. Limited by the number of aircraft its carriers could hold, the Royal Navy concentrated on procuring machines that could fill multiple roles (bomber, torpedo-bomber, long-range scout, gunfire spotting etc.) like the Fairey Swordfish, Albacore and Blackburn Skua. An aircraft that performed exclusively as a fighter was last on the list.

In September 1939, the Fleet Air Arm was equipped with 232 operational aircraft. In the majority was the fabric-covered Swordfish torpedo scout bomber. The only modern aircraft on strength were 30 Skuas. The latter was designed as a fighter/dive-bomber, but was more accurately a poor dive-bomber. Along with 18 biplane

Sea Gladiators (adapted from the land-based version), they made up the entire fighter force available to the Royal Navy at the start of World War II.

Operations during the German invasion of Norway and subsequent actions in the Mediterranean against the Italians showed that the Fleet Air Arm did not have a fighter capable of engaging Axis fighters, or bombers for that matter. As a result, the Royal Navy quickly accepted a number of Hawker Hurricanes and transformed them into Sea Hurricanes through the fitment of an arrestor hook. This proved to the powers that be that high-performance shore-based fighters could operate from a carrier deck. While the Sea Hurricane was a success, the limits of its performance were soon exposed. What was needed was a fast, agile fighter, and the Admiralty soon demanded Spitfires.

The idea of operating a Spitfire from a carrier deck was met with mixed feelings by Fleet Air Arm pilots. While many admired the Spitfire, and were more than happy to fly one, they questioned how it would realistically perform from a pitching carrier deck. Despite being a weapon of war, the Spitfire could, ironically, be described as elegant, and when asked to fly from an aircraft carrier, as fragile. Could its slender fuselage and narrow-track undercarriage stand up to the harsh deceleration of an arrested landing? What about its landing speed and view from the cockpit over its long nose? The difficulties were many, but the urgency of war pushed those worries aside, and soon the 'Sea Spitfire' would take to the air.

The first Spitfire to be 'hooked' was Mk VB BL676 in late 1941. An A-frame arrestor hook was attached to the bottom longerons and slinging points were introduced on the centre longerons. During the Christmas week of 1941, Lt Cdr H. P. Bramwell made 12 successful deck landings, seven take-offs and four catapult launches from the fleet carrier HMS *Illustrious*. Bramwell's report was encouraging enough for the Admiralty, and soon 250 Spitfire Mk VBs and VCs were earmarked for conversion. The first to be delivered would be 48 existing, but modified, Mk VBs, with the remaining 202 being new production Mk VCs.

Adaptation for shipboard use was a very simple matter. Naval HF (high frequency) R/T (Radio Telephone), IFF (Identification Friend or Foe) and homing beacon receivers were fitted, along with a hydraulically damped A-frame arrestor hook and slinging points. The Mk VBs became Seafire IBs and the Mk VCs were designated as Seafire IICs. The only difference between the Mk IB and IIC was in the wing. The Mk VB was fitted with the 'B' wing, which could accommodate one 20mm Hispano cannon (120 rounds) and two Browning 0.303-in machine guns (350 rounds per gun), with a firing time of between 10 and 12 seconds. The 'C' wing was designed to carry two 20mm cannons or one 20mm cannon and two machine guns. The extra weight associated with two additional 20mm cannons proved to be unacceptable, and the 'C' wing was therefore never used. The Seafire's built in armament remained unchanged during the war at two cannons and four machine guns.

With the modifications complete, the new Seafire's overall weight rose by only five percent, and maximum speed was only reduced by 5–6 mph. It was a good start.

The Seafire IB was viewed as an interim model only, and a grand total of 211 were produced. The majority was assigned to Nos 1 and 2 Naval Fighter Schools at Yeovilton and Henstridge, while others served with the School of Naval Air Warfare.

HMS *Fledgling*, in Staffordshire, in 1944–45 was home to one of the Women's Royal Naval Service aircraft maintenance training courses. This evocative colour photograph shows a rather well-worn Seafire I with its cannon armament removed. It also reveals just how many types of fighters the Royal Navy employed during World War II (the most by any navy). We can see a Corsair, two Wildcats, two Sea Hurricanes and a Fulmar, as well as two Barracudas.
(DND Canadian Archives)

OPPOSITE
Seafire III NN212 was flown in combat by Sub-Lt Gerry 'Spud' Murphy on the last day of the war, when he used it to obtain his only aerial victories of the war. He had earlier seen action in the aircraft off the Sakishima Gunto Islands during Operations *Iceberg I* and *II* in the spring of 1945.

The only frontline squadron to be completely equipped with the Seafire IB was 801 NAS, which served aboard the old Fleet carrier HMS *Furious* from October 1942 through to September 1944.

The Seafire IIC was the first purpose-built naval fighter to enter Fleet Air Arm service. While the Seafire IBs had been conversions of Spitfire VB airframes, the 372 Seafire IIC/L IICs that followed were purpose built on the production line for naval service. The primary difference between the Mk IB and Mk IIC was the addition of catapult spools. This required strengthening around the spools, but the most significant beefing up took the form of an external fishplate. This ran along the line of the mid fuselage longeron, between the forward cockpit bulkhead and radio bay.

This additional strengthening and installation resulted in even more weight being added to the fighter. Compensating balance weights then had to be added to restore the fighter's centre-of-gravity to acceptable limits. Add in 25lbs of armour, the heavier 'C' wing and the strengthened undercarriage, and the Mk IIC's empty weight rose by an additional six percent over that of the Mk IB. Equipped with the same Merlin 45 or 46 as the latter, the Mk IIC proved to be 15mph slower than the Mk IB.

Operation *Torch* in North Africa in November 1942 was the first Allied amphibious assault to enjoy carrier-borne cooperation between the US and Royal Navies. It was also the first time that the Seafire was used in combat, but the results were mixed. Four squadrons were equipped with Mk IICs and one, 801 NAS, used

30ft 2.5in.

8ft 0in.

36ft 10in.

Prototype Seafire III MA970 was converted from the first production Seafire IIC. This variant flew for the first time during the second week of November 1942. The folding wing mechanisms were quite simple, with the first break just inboard of the inner cannon bay and the second near the tip of the wing between the mainplane and wing tip. (ww2images.com)

the Mk IB. They flew 180 sorties and shot down three aircraft, damaged three others in the air and destroyed four on the ground. However, no fewer than 21 Seafires were lost, but only three as a result of enemy action. These operational losses were mainly due to the extremely poor visibility in thick haze on the first day of operations.

Despite the Seafire IIC proving to be slower than the Mk IB, its combat performance had been deemed successful, although there was concern over its shortcomings. Initial rate of climb and low-altitude speed left something to be desired, and in an effort to rectify these problems the aircraft was fitted with a Merlin 32 engine, which boasted a cropped supercharger impeller to boost the powerplant's performance closer to the ground.

While the Seafire IB and IIC (with their Rolls-Royce Merlin 45 and 46 engines) had been designed as medium to high-altitude fighters, the majority of interceptions involving Fleet Air Arm aircraft in the European theatre took place below 10,000ft. As if to prove this point, the first three interceptions of Ju 88s by Seafire IBs proved disappointing when the British fighters failed to catch the nimble German bombers that had attacked at low level.

At the end of 1942 it was decided that the Mk IIC should be re-engined with the Merlin 32, which produced 1,640hp at 1,750ft. To take advantage of the increased horsepower, a four-bladed propeller was fitted. With a new engine and propeller, the Seafire L IIC was born.

Legendary British test pilot Capt Eric Brown was deeply involved with the testing of the Seafire. Here, he describes his experience with the new Seafire L IIC in a quote taken from the *Air International* (Volume 15, Number 3) article 'Spitfires with Sea Legs':

The Seafire L Mk IIC was the most exciting aircraft that I had flown to that time. Its initial rate of climb and acceleration were little short of magnificent, and at maximum boost it could maintain 4,600ft/min up to 6,000ft. Another result of the installation of the Merlin 32 was a quite dramatic reduction in take-off distance and, in fact, the L Mk IIC without flap could get airborne in a shorter distance than the standard Mk IIC using full flap! My enthusiasm for this new Seafire variant was such that, one afternoon, in sheer exhilaration, I looped it around both spans of the Forth Bridge in succession – court martial stuff nowadays, but during a war nobody has the time to bother with such formalities.

The result of Capt Eric Brown's flight tests led to the decision to convert all Mk IICs to L Mk IIC configuration. A sub-type of the Seafire L IIC was the LR IIC, which was a fighter-reconnaissance aircraft. Two cameras were fitted and full cannon and machine gun armament was retained. It is believed that about 30 aircraft were modified for the fighter/reconnaissance role. Although the L Mk IIC was progressively replaced by the F Mk III, its performance was, in many respects, better than the later machine, and it was not until the very end of 1944 that the Seafire L IIC was finally supplanted in frontline service.

After the quick invasion of Sicily in 1943, and with the knowledge that Italy was negotiating a separate armistice, the Allies swiftly drew up a plan for an amphibious assault in the Bay of Salerno on 9 September 1943. It was here that the Allies believed they could cut Italy in half and drive on to Naples. It was also where the Seafire earned its negative reputation.

Carrier-based air cover for the invasion was essential. Airfields in Sicily were 220 to 240 miles from the landing beaches, and while 2,000 land-based fighters were available, they would be unable to provide more than 36 aircraft with a patrol time of between 20 to 40 minutes, depending on the type, over the invasion fleet. The Seafire, even with its short legs, could provide more than an hour of patrol time. For the invasion, the Royal Navy brought 121 Seafires to battle – 15 Mk IICs and 106 L Mk IICs. All of the latter were embarked in four small escort (HMS *Attacker*, *Battler*, *Hunter* and *Stalker*) and two fleet (HMS *Formidable* and *Illustrious*) carriers.

While the landings at Salerno were ultimately successful, the reputation afforded the Seafire was not. Statistically, the numbers were grim. Although only two Seafires were lost in action, just two enemy aircraft had been destroyed. In all, 42 Seafires were lost or written off in accidents, which amounted to one aircraft destroyed or seriously damaged for every ninth sortie flown. The reasons for the Seafire's poor performance were two fold – operating conditions and pilot inexperience. Many of the pilots had never flown off a small escort carrier before, and the lack of wind meant an increase in approach speeds of 10 to 15 knots. But when one looks closely at the sortie rate per serviceable aircraft, the Seafire did very well. It went from 2.5 to 4.1 sorties per serviceable aircraft and, in the process, protected the fleet by forcing enemy aircraft to turn back or jettison their bombs prematurely.

The next Seafire variants to see service in World War II were the F Mk III and L Mk III – the first to feature folding wings. The F Mk III was equipped with the Merlin 55 engine and a four-bladed propeller. The 'C' wing was further modified through the elimination of the outboard cannon bay and blast tube stub. The Merlin 55 had an automatic boost control and barometric governing, which relieved the pilot of the need to use his judgment to get the most out of his engine. These modifications resulted in an aircraft superior to the Mk IIC. The F Mk III was 20mph faster at all heights, with an increase in rate of climb. Below 10,000ft, it was still inferior to the Mk IIC, however, but the F Mk III was built as a medium to high-level fighter, so this was of no great concern.

Only 103 F Mk IIIs were built before production switched to the L Mk III, and 887 NAS would be the only unit equipped with this variant through to war's end.

Legendary US Navy test pilot 'Corky' Meyer, who attended the Joint USAAF/US Navy Fighter Conference of March 1943 at Eglin Army airfield, in Florida, had the chance to fly an early Seafire F III at this event:

Without argument, the Spitfire/Seafire configuration was probably the most beautiful fighter ever to emerge from a drawing board. Its elliptical wing and long, slim fuselage were visually most delightful, and its flight characteristics equalled its aerodynamic beauty.

The Seafire had such delightful upright flying qualities that knowing it had an inverted fuel and oil system, I decided to try inverted 'figure-8s'. They were as easy as pie, even when hanging by the complicated, but comfortable, British pilot restraint harness. I was surprised to hear myself laughing as if I were crazy. I have never enjoyed a flight in a fighter as much before or since, or felt so comfortable in an aeroplane at any flight attitude. It was clear to see how so few exhausted, hastily trained, Battle of Britain pilots were able to fight off Hitler's hordes for so long, and so successfully, with it.

The Lend-Lease Royal Navy Wildcats, Hellcats and Corsair fighters were only workhorses. The Seafire III was a dashing stallion!

The final Merlin-engined version to see service, and the one built in the greatest numbers, was the L Mk III. First flown in the autumn of 1943, it was the logical successor to the L Mk IIC. The only difference between the F Mk III and L Mk III was the substitution of the Merlin 55 with the 55M. Like the Merlin 32, this engine was optimised for low-level performance through the fitment of a cropped supercharger impeller that helped the powerplant deliver 1,585hp at 2,750ft. Later model L Mk IIIs would receive a minor armament change when the Mk V version of the 20mm Hispano cannon replaced the Mk II. It was a lighter weapon with a shorter barrel. The 'C' wing was also modified to carry two rocket-projectile launchers under each main plane. A photo-reconnaissance version was also produced as the FR Mk III (129 built).

The L Mk III and FR Mk III were the most successful Seafire variants, and were built in the greatest numbers – 808 completed by Westland Aircraft Limited and 252 by Cunliffe-Owen Aircraft Limited.

When the Royal Navy committed carriers to the Indian and Pacific theatres in 1944, close to a third of the entire fighter force available was made up of Seafire F IIIs and L IIIs. With the Fleet Air Arm also operating a mixed force of American-built Hellcats and Corsairs, the Seafire would be relegated to short-range Combat Air Patrols and anti-submarine patrols. Only when drop tanks were made available did the Seafires participate in escort and strike operations against targets on the Japanese home islands.

It was here that the Seafire pilots of the Fleet Air Arm would meet the remnants of the once powerful JAAF and IJNAF. In the last desperate battles of the war, the Seafire would compile a small but impressive score, and participate in the war's last dogfight between British and Japanese aircraft.

A6M ZERO-SEN

Any discussion of Japanese aircraft in World War II must begin with the Mitsubishi A6M Reisen (Zero-sen being the rough translation). It formed the backbone of Japanese naval fighter forces from the beginning of the war right up until the end.

In mid 1937 the IJNAF issued specifications for a new fighter – 12-Shi – that were far in excess of those of the A5M 'Claude' that was just beginning to enter service. The IJNAF wanted a fighter capable of intercepting and destroying enemy bombers, and to serve as an escort fighter with a combat performance greater than that of enemy interceptors. It was a tall order, but the war against China accelerated the development of Japan's air arm.

Japanese success with the nimble 'Claude' reinforced a strong belief among IJNAF pilots in the continuing need for a highly manoeuvrable fighter designed for tight-turning air-to-air combat. The lessons learned in China would not serve the new fighter well. The belief that a light, nimble aircraft would dominate the skies was misplaced. The Allies had learned that manoeuvrability was the least important attribute when it came to fighter design.

Japanese designers were also highly influenced by their pilots, especially those of the IJNAF's Yokosuka Naval Air Corps. Requirements for the new fighter were revealed to representatives of Nakajima and Mitsubishi at Yokosuka on 17 January 1938. Nakajima quickly withdrew, convinced the job was not possible. Mitsubishi at the time was in the process of developing the IJNAF's 11-Shi bomber, and it was therefore extremely hesitant to invest resources into something that showed little hope of success. The company was persuaded to accept the project, however, and in exchange it was allowed to drop the 11-Shi bomber project. Under these strict circumstances Mitsubishi designer Hiro Horikoshi and his team created a minor miracle.

In order to produce what was in essence a 'super Claude', the Zero was designed to be as light as possible. The wing was built as one piece, and it made use of a unique lightweight material called Extra-Super Duralumin.

Engine power was another important factor in the new fighter's outstanding performance. At the time Japanese engine manufacturers were only producing powerplants in the 800–1,000hp range. There were a number of advanced engines in the design and experimental stages, but to move the project forward Horikoshi and his team needed a reliable one. At the time there were three available – the 875hp Mitsubishi Zuisei 13, the 950hp Nakajima Sakae 12 and the 1,070hp Mitsubishi Kinsei 46. The first two prototypes would be fitted with the Zuisei 13 engine, and the Sakae 12 was installed in the third prototype. The latter produced better performance than the Mitsubishi engine, and it would duly power the Zero-sen through its entire combat career.

Saddled with an engine that developed just 950hp, Horikoshi had little choice but to dispense with anything that added unnecessary weight and drag. Items such as armour plate and self-sealing fuel tanks were out of the question.

The Zero-sen symbolised both Japan's military success and its inability to fight a protracted conflict with a major power. So it was a bad omen when, on 23 March 1939, the Zero-sen prototype had to be taken apart at the Mitsubishi plant, loaded onto two oxcarts and moved some 25 miles to the naval air base at Kagamigahara for its first flight. Powered by an 875hp Mitsubishi Zuisei 13 engine, the new A6M1 prototype took to the air for the first time on 1 April 1939. Production models of the Zero-sen would be powered by the Nakajima Sakae 12 engine, rated at 950hp at

This Nakajima Sakae 12 radial engine was taken from the first Zero-sen to be captured intact and flight-tested by US forces – the A6M2 was discovered in the Aleutian Islands in July 1942. The 14-cylinder twin row radial produced just 950hp, which did not compare well with the engines that powered Allied fighters at the time. The Merlin 45 fitted to the first Seafires in December 1941 developed 1,415hp at 11,000ft. (Naval Historical Center)

take-off. The IJNAF subsequently took delivery of the second prototype on 25 October 1939, and less than a year later, on the last day of July 1940, the Zero-sen entered frontline service.

Aerodynamically, the A6M was extremely efficient. Saburo Sakai, who was Japan's highest scoring surviving ace at war's end, described the Zero-sen thus:

The Zero excited me as nothing else had ever done. Even on the ground it had the cleanest lines I had ever seen in an aeroplane. It was a dream to fly.

Because of its low weight relative to engine power, clean design and high lift, the Zero-sen was one of the most manoeuvrable fighters of World War II. At low speeds it could turn inside any Allied fighter with ease. It also had a nasty bite, however. Many historians have listed the many advanced performance qualities of the A6M, but what is sometimes overlooked is the selection of armament. Boasting two license-built 20mm Oerlikon cannons and two Type 97 7.7mm machines guns, the Zero-sen packed a powerful punch. Fitting the fighter with cannon was a bold step forward, and one that would soon be followed by the Allies.

The fighter's light weight had another benefit – range. The Zero-sen was extremely fuel-efficient, and as a result it had a range of more than 1,100 miles. During the battle for Guadalcanal in August 1942, the A6M was the only fighter in the world at the time that could fly the 560 miles from Rabual to Guadalcanal.

The first Zero-sens to experience combat were those assigned to the 12th Rengo Kokutai (Combined Naval Air Corps) in China. This force was made up of 15 pre-production A6M2 Model 11s. On 13 September 1940, 13 fighters escorted a small force of bombers sent to attack the city of Chungking. As the Japanese aircraft left the target area, Chinese fighters appeared. The Zero-sens quickly turned around and pounced on the mixed force of Soviet-built Polikarpov I-15 biplanes and I-16 monoplane fighters. In the one-sided battle that ensued, no fewer than 27 Chinese aircraft were shot down.

After a year of combat, the small force of Zero-sens had chalked up an impressive score – 354 sorties, 44 enemy aircraft shot down and 62 damaged for the loss of two A6M2s to anti-aircraft fire. The extreme confidence generated by the Zero-sen's initial success gave IJNAF commanders an unshakable faith in the aircraft, and belief that their future military operations would be nothing but successful.

When war broke out in the Pacific, the Japanese had approximately 400 A6M2 Model 21 Zero-sens on strength, of which 108 took part in the attack on Pearl Harbor on 7 December 1941. It was an incredibly small number of fighters with which to start a war, but Japanese commanders believed the Zero-sen to be the equal of two to five enemy fighters.

The Type 3 13.2mm machine gun greatly enhanced the Zero-sen's hitting power. The A6M5c Type 52c was armed with three of these weapons, along with two Type 99 20mm cannon. The Type 3 was basically a copy of the American M2 Browning 0.50-cal machine gun, but it fired 13.2mm Hotchkiss cartridges. Rate-of-fire was 800 rounds per minute, with a muzzle velocity of 2,610ft per second. (National Archives)

The Model 21 was the same as the Model 11 except for its folding wing tips. Carrier trials had shown that the Zero-sen was a snug fit while riding the elevator between the hanger and flightdeck. Each folding wing tip was 20 inches in length. Had the entire wing been made to fold, Japanese carriers could have carried considerably more A6Ms, but it would have increased the weight of the fighter and thus seriously degraded its overall performance.

The appearance of the Zero-sen came as a complete and utter surprise to both the Americans and the British. They were also completely unaware of its astonishing performance capabilities. Observers in China had passed their observations along, but these were ignored. Allied ignorance was complete. Their lack of knowledge, or stubborn racist belief that the Japanese could not possibly produce a fighter like the Zero-sen, led them to believe that its genius was imitative. When US fighters proved unable to cope with the A6M, embarrassed government officials were quick to claim that the Mitsubishi fighter was in fact a copy of an American design. Once that was accepted, the Zero-sen was considered to be a good fighter!

The major variants of the Zero that would see extensive combat during World War II were the A6M2 Model 21 (740 built), A6M3 Model 32 (343 built), A6M5 Model 52 (approximately 5,000 built, including all sub-variants) and A6M7 Model 63 (exact number built unknown).

During the early months of the war, the A6M2 Model 21 ruled the skies. From Pearl Harbor to the Philippines, Wake Island to Australia, the Zero-sen established a reputation like no other. Its phenomenal range caused great confusion and consternation among American commanders. The day following the attack on Pearl Harbor, Clark Field, in the Philippines, was savaged by Japanese bombers escorted by Zero-sens of the Tainan Kokutai. The Americans were convinced that the fighters had been launched from a nearby aircraft carrier. In fact these A6M2s were operating from bases on Formosa – a round trip of 900 nautical miles.

For nearly six months Japanese military expansion went unchecked. It was not until the Battle of the Coral Sea on 7–8 May 1942 that the Zero-sen and the IJN first tasted defeat. The following month, on 4–5 June, the Japanese suffered a catastrophic reversal that proved to be a major turning point in the war. The battle of Midway pitted four Japanese carriers against three American 'flattops'. When the engagement was over the Japanese had lost all four carriers, 234 aircraft and more than ten percent of its veteran fighter pilots. It was a stunning loss.

In order to make good this pilot attrition, the IJNAF recalled many veterans from land-based units across the empire back to Japan to serve as instructors. Flight training was shortened and entrance requirements were lowered in order to make up the numbers. These factors ultimately combined to start a process that would produce pilots that were ill equipped for frontline combat flying come 1944.

In October 1942, the next major variant of the Zero-sen appeared. To compete with the expected increase in performance in Allied fighters, the A6M's altitude and climb performance had to be improved. Additional power was added with the fitment of the new Sakae 21 engine, which delivered 1,100hp. The new engine had a change in reduction gearing that allowed for a larger propeller, and it also

OPPOSITE
Lt Yutaka Morioka embodied the fighter pilot spirit, and at the age of just 23 he was the youngest IJNAF squadron leader. Indeed, he was in charge of three squadrons – two equipped with Raidens and one with Zero-sens. He preferred to fly the A6M5c/7 rather than the more modern, and faster, J2M3, and just two hours before the end of the war he became an ace whilst at the controls of this aircraft when he downed an F6F-5 Hellcat of VBF-88 over Tokyo Bay.

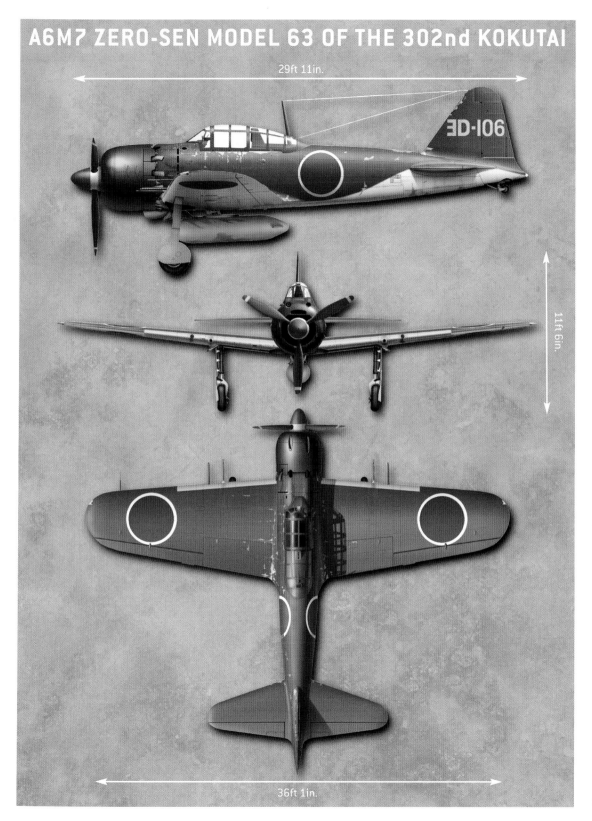

29ft 11in.

11ft 6in.

36ft 1in.

This captured A6M5 was operated by the Technical Air Intelligence Center, based at Ontario Army Air Corps Base, California, in late 1944. By this stage of the war the Zero-sen's 'secrets' were well known, and this particular example was probably used to help train new aircrew with aircraft identification, and to show them what they would be up against once posted to the Pacific theatre. (Author's collection)

incorporated a two-speed supercharger. Despite the increase in power, the Zero-sen's performance remained relatively the same, however. During flight tests, pilots recommended removing the folding wing tips. The new squared-off wing variant was designated the A6M3 Model 32 – it was code named 'Hamp' by the Allies.

The defeats would continue unabated. As the Allies introduced better fighters with greater speed and firepower, the A6M could not keep up. New models were introduced, but by the end of the war the Zero-sen remained essentially the same aircraft. By 1945, most units were equipped with the A6M5 Model 52 and its sub-variants, the 52a, 52b and 52c. The new model, introduced in the summer of 1943, was designed to improve the rate at which Zero-sens could be produced.

All four were powered by the Sakae 21 engine, developing just 1,130hp. Capable of increased speeds in a dive, the fighter's performance was also improved through the replacement of the previous model's exhaust collector ring with straight individual stacks – the high velocity exhaust gas was directed backward for additional thrust. In the end, the new Model 52 had a top speed of just 351mph at 19,700ft, which was only a 20mph increase over the Model 21. The Model 52 was the most widely used A6M variant of them all.

In experienced hands the fabled Zero-sen was still a deadly foe even in 1945, but in the final months of the war the once fearsome A6M was turned into something even more desperate – the kamikaze.

TECHNICAL
SPECIFICATIONS

SEAFIRE

In the early autumn of 1941 the Admiralty was painfully aware of its deficiencies when it came to fielding a modern carrier-based interceptor. As fighter production made up for the losses following the Battle of Britain, the Air Ministry finally agreed to release Hurricanes for Fleet Air Arm use. While the Sea Hurricane proved capable, it was not the answer. A new naval interceptor in the form of the Blackburn Firebrand was under development, but it would not be ready for production until late 1943 at the earliest – in actuality, the first production aircraft did not fly until May 1945! The Grumman F4F Wildcat began reaching the fleet in small numbers in late 1940, but its design 'stretch' was limited. It was time to add a hook to the Spitfire and turn it into the Seafire.

PROTOTYPE SEAFIRE BL676

Production Spitfire VB BL676 (fitted with a chin-mounted tropical filter) was modified through the fitment of an A-frame arrestor hook attached to the bottom longerons of its fuselage. Underfuselage slinging points were also introduced by Vickers-Supermarine to the centre longerons aft of the fighter's engine firewall and at the rear of its cockpit. The aircraft was subsequently modified to full Seafire IB specification.

SEAFIRE IB

Forty-eight existing Mk VB airframes were converted into Seafire IBs, some of which were themselves remanufactured Spitfire Is. The aircraft were fitted with A-frame arrestor hooks, released via a Bowden cable, and slinging points, with necessary local strengthening. The Seafire IB also boasted naval HF R/T, IFF and the Type 72 homing beacon. The fighter's empty weight rose by only five percent, however. Power was provided by either a Rolls-Royce Merlin 45 or 46 engine rated at 1,415hp. Armament consisted of four 0.303-in Browning machine guns with 350 rounds per gun and two 20mm Hispano Mk 2 cannons with 120 rounds per gun (armament would remain the same for all marks for the entire war). Air Service Training Limited produced 48 Mk IBs and Cunliffe-Owen Aircraft Limited was responsible for 118 examples. A further 45 Spitfires were 'hooked' at RAF Maintenance Units, with associated R/T and IFF modifications also being carried out, but no slinging points or homing beacons were added.

SEAFIRE IIC

The Seafire IIC was built from the outset as a naval fighter. Mk VC airframes on the production line were converted by Vickers-Supermarine and the rest were built from the ground up by Westland Aircraft Limited. The latter was also given responsibility for the further development of the Merlin-engined Seafire series. Naval modifications were the same as for the Mk IB, but with the addition of catapult spools for the first time. Strengthening had to be provided around the spools, with the most significant visual difference being the external fishplate that ran along the line of the mid-fuselage longeron between the forward cockpit bulkhead and the radio bay. Empty weight rose by another six percent over the Mk IB without any increase in engine power – the Merlin 45/46 was retained. Increased drag from the catapult spools alone accounted for a drop of 7mph. The extra weight of the universal 'C' wing and an additional

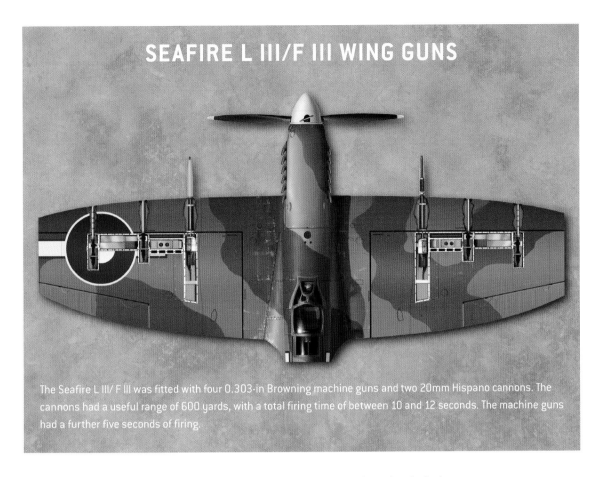

SEAFIRE L III/F III WING GUNS

The Seafire L III/ F III was fitted with four 0.303-in Browning machine guns and two 20mm Hispano cannons. The cannons had a useful range of 600 yards, with a total firing time of between 10 and 12 seconds. The machine guns had a further five seconds of firing.

25lbs of armour plate resulted in the main undercarriage being strengthened and raked forward by two inches. As a result, the Mk IIC was 15mph slower at all heights than the Mk IB. The strengthened undercarriage allowed the Mk IIC to carry a 45 imperial gallon jettisonable 'slipper' tank or 500lb bomb. The first Seafire IIC flew on 28 May 1943 and was delivered on 15 June.

SEAFIRE L IIC

While the Seafire was designed as a medium to high-level fighter, the majority of naval interceptions in the European theatre took place below 10,000ft. While the Rolls-Royce Merlin 45 gave its maximum power at 13,000ft, and the Merlin 46 at 20,000ft, it was clear a new engine was required. At the end of 1942 it was decided that all aircraft with the Merlin 46 would be re-engined with the Merlin 32. The latter possessed a smaller, cropped supercharger impeller that added more power to the propeller instead of being used to provide more airflow for operations at high altitudes. Full throttle output at 3,000ft rose by 430hp to 1,640hp. To take advantage of the increase in power, a four-bladed Rotol propeller was fitted, replacing the three-blade unit that had been standard to the Mk IIC and IB. The Seafire L IIC had outstanding low-level performance, and its rate of climb and initial acceleration were far better than any other naval fighter produced during the war. The L Mk IIC, at maximum emergency boost, could climb at 4,600ft per minute up to 6,000ft, and could reach 20,000ft a full two minutes ahead of the Mk IIC. This was some 1,500ft per minute better than the Corsair or Hellcat. Maximum speed was 316mph at sea level and 335mph at 6,000ft. Later, some LIICs had their wing tips clipped to increase their rate of roll. This slightly increased maximum speed, but landing and take-off runs were longer. In many respects the L Mk IIC variant was the best Seafire of the war. Some 262 Mk IICs and L Mk IICs were built by Vickers-Supermarine and 110 by Westland Aircraft Limited.

SEAFIRE LR IIC

In 1943 a number of Seafire L IICs were modified along the lines of the photo-reconnaissance Spitfire PR XIII (itself based on the Spitfire VII). While the latter was equipped with three cameras, the LR Mk IIC had only two F24 type cameras due to the position of the arrestor hook. The Seafire LR IIC entered frontline service with No 4 Naval Fighter Wing in late 1943, each of its three squadrons being equipped with between two and five aircraft. Unlike the PR XIII, the LR Mk IIC retained the full cannon and machine gun armament. There are no records of how many conversions were made, but about 30 aircraft are believed to have been produced.

SEAFIRE F III

From the very beginning, the Royal Navy was keen for a folding wing version of the Seafire to be built. The Corsair and Hellcat were due to enter service during the second half of 1943, but competition from the US Navy and Marine Corps created a degree of uncertainty regarding a secure supply of aircraft. In order to permit unrestricted

This unidentified Mk III Seafire banks towards the camera, its British Pacific Fleet markings clearly visible on the uppersurface of its port wing and fuselage – note the old roundel on the starboard wing, however. These were adopted in April 1945, and were designed 'to be similar to those used in the insignia of the United States Navy.' The official dimensions for these BPF markings were based on two sizes – 32- or 48-in in diameter roundel. The 32- and 48-in roundels proved to be either too small or too big for the Seafire's slim fuselage, so a semi-official 40-in diameter roundel was applied instead. (Phil Jarrett)

frontline service on all of Her Majesty's carriers, the Seafire needed a folding wing. The first production Mk IIC was duly pulled from the production line and used for the development of the folding wing Mk III. The folding system was simple enough, and consisted of one break just inboard of the inner cannon bay and a second at the wing tip. No power-assist folding was ever considered due to weight restrictions, and in the end the new wing added just 125lbs per aircraft. It was also at this point that the Seafire would consolidate its armament. This allowed the 'C' wing to be modified internally, with both the outboard cannon bays and the blast-tube stubs being deleted. The Martin-Baker Patent Belt-Fed Mechanism was also adapted. This unit had a lower profile than that of the original, and as a consequence, the large wing blisters over the feed mechanisms were replaced by small teardrop fairings. These two modifications added close to 10mph to the fighter's top speed. The F Mk III was also given a different engine in the shape of the Merlin 55. It had the same output as the Merlin 45, but was more efficient due to the automatic boost control and barometric governing of the 'full throttle height'. The Merlin 55, along with a cleaner wing and four-bladed propeller, increased the F Mk III's speed by 20mph at all heights over the Mk IIC. Between 3,000ft and 14,000ft, the Seafire F III was faster than the F6F-3 Hellcat, and was evenly matched with the F4U-1A from 6,000ft to 10,000ft. The F Mk III was designed to fight at heights between 8,000ft and 15,000ft, thus making it a true medium-level fighter. Westland built a total of 103 F Mk IIIs.

Boasting a mix of blue and sky propeller spinners, Seafire IIIs from 801 and 880 NASs run their engines up on the deck of HMS *Implacable* as the vessel turns into wind prior to launching its air wing in early August 1945. Note that all of the Seafires are fitted with ex-P-40 drop tanks. 828 NAS's Avengers are 'chocked and chained' on the stern of the carrier. (Author's Collection)

SEAFIRE L III

First flown in the autumn of 1943, the L Mk III version of the Seafire would be produced in the greatest numbers. The logical successor to the L Mk IIC, the new version was identical to the F Mk III except that it was powered by the Rolls-Royce Merlin 55M engine. While the latter had slightly less power than the Merlin 32 (1,585hp for the 55M at 2,750ft versus 1,640hp at 1,750ft for the 32), the new L Mk III was actually faster in level flight. The fastest of all the Merlin-engined Seafires, the L Mk III was capable of 358mph at 6,000ft, and in 1945 it was still the fastest and steepest climbing Allied carrier interceptor. Later production L Mk IIIs received the Hispano Mk V cannon. This was a lighter weapon with a shorter barrel. The final version of the L Mk III was the FR Mk III. It was basically the same as the LR Mk IIC, but with a slight difference in the camera installation. Some 129 aircraft of this type were built by Cunliffe-Owen. In total, 1,060 L Mk IIIs and FR Mk IIIs were constucted by Westland Aircraft Limited and Cunliffe-Owen Aircraft Limited.

A6M ZERO-SEN

The Mitsubishi A6M Zero-sen was undoubtedly the best carrier fighter until the advent of the F6F Hellcat in late 1943. Its introduction and early aerial victories were impressive. During the first year of the war, A6M2s and A6M3s were as fast or faster than most Allied fighters in the Pacific (mainly P-36 Hawks, P-39 Airacobras, P-40 Warhawks, F2A Buffaloes, F4F Wildcats and Hurricanes). The Zero-sen's early success was due in large part to the well-trained pilots who flew it. Typically, most IJNAF aviators by the time of Pearl Harbor averaged some 800 flying hours apiece, and many had extensive combat experience from China. As the war progressed the A6M's fighting qualities began to deteriorate, and so did the quality of its pilots.

MITSUBISHI 12-SHI (A6M1)

This designation applied to the first two prototypes powered by the 875hp Mitsubishi Zuisei engine. Armament consisted of two 7.7mm machine guns and two 20mm cannon. Top speed was 304mph at 12,470ft.

A6M2 MODEL 11

The third prototype was powered by the more powerful 950hp Nakajima Sakae engine. Production started in December 1939, and it was the first model to see combat in China. A total of 64 were built.

A6M2 MODEL 21

The Model 11 proved itself in combat in China and performed well during carrier trials, but its snug fit while riding on carrier elevators proved a problem. The possible damage to the wing tips resulted in these sections being made to fold manually. This reduced the span by 20 inches, and warranted a new designation. The Nakajima Aircraft Company began manufacturing the Zero-sen in November 1941, and along with Mitsubishi produced 740 A6M2s. This particular variant was given the Allied code name 'Zeke 21'.

A6M2s of *Shokaku's* fighter squadron run up as the carrier sails into wind for the dawn launch northeast of Hawaii on 7 December 1941. Six Zero-sens from this unit participated in the first wave attack, strafing Kaneohe and Bellows airfields. (via Aerospace Publishing)

A6M3 MODEL 32

To improve the Zero-sen's altitude and climb performance, the fighter was fitted with the Nakajima NK1F Sakae 21 engine, which boasted a two-speed supercharger – the powerplant was rated at 1,100hp. The engine alone added an extra 280lbs in weight over the Model 21, and fuel capacity was also reduced by 21 gallons due to the increase in the dimensional size of the NK1F Sakae 21. Tactical combat radius suffered considerably because of the difference in fuel capacity combined with the new engine's consumption at full power. Even with the improved powerplant, the performance gains were negligible. Test pilots flying the new model suggested removing the folding wing tips, and the squared-wing model did indeed have an improved maximum speed, but little else. When the A6M3 was first encountered in combat in October 1942, it was given the code name 'Hamp', which was subsequently changed to 'Zeke 32'. Ammunition for the 20mm cannon was increased from 60 to 100 rounds per gun. Some 343 were delivered to the IJNAF.

A6M3a Model 22s of the 251st Kokutai head out on patrol from Rabaul in 1943. This particular fighter was routinely flown by veteran 86-kill ace WO Hiroyoshi Nishizawa, and it is seen here carrying a 330-litre drop tank. (via Aerospace Publishing)

A6M3 MODEL 22

This aircraft actually preceded the Model 32, but in order to meet the demand for a squared wing version its production was delayed. The Model 22 was built simply because the IJNAF needed to claw back the lost range due to the reduced wing area of the Model 32. Although the Sakae 21 engine was retained, the fighter's fuel capacity was increased by 24 US gallons. This gave the Model 22 the greatest range of all the Zero-sen variants, and it arrived in the frontline just in time to fly the 560 nautical miles from Rabaul to the combat zone over Guadalcanal in August 1942.

A6M5 MODEL 52

By late 1943 the Zero-sen's poor performance against newer Allied fighters like the F4U Corsair, P-38 Lightning and Spitfire was clear to both the Allies and the Japanese. Promises of a new interceptor did not materialise, and the Japanese were forced to modify the existing A6M3. The Model 52 was designed to simplify and speed up production, as well as to increase its diving speed. Wingspan remained the same as the square tip Model 32, but modifications included the elimination of the wing tip folding mechanism. To increase diving speed, heavy-gauge wing skinning was added and the exhaust collector ring was replaced with straight individual stacks. This directed high velocity exhaust gas backward for additional thrust. Maximum speed reached 351mph in level flight at 19,000ft. The A6M5 Model 52 was the most widely used model, with 1,701 manufactured.

A6M5a MODEL 52a

Heavier-gauge wing skin was added to increase diving speed to 460mph – just 20mph slower than the F4U Corsair. This was to be the highest diving speed attained by any Zero-sen variant. Firepower was improved with the addition of new Type 99 Model 2 Mk 4 20mm cannons. Mitsubishi produced 391 examples. The total built by Nakajima is unknown.

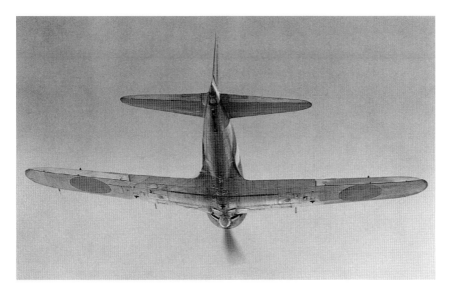

A6M5b MODEL 52b

CO_2 fire extinguishers were built into the fuel tank areas of the fuselage and around the firewall. Pilot protection was increased with the addition of a 5mm bullet resistant windscreen and firepower was also improved for the first time when one of the two Type 97 7.7mm fuselage machine guns was replaced by a larger Type 3 13mm machine gun. Mitsubishi produced 470 examples.

A6M5c MODEL 52c

Increased firepower, more fuel and pilot protection. The Model 52c's armament was increased to three Type 3 13mm machines guns (one fuselage-mounted and two in the wings) and two 20mm cannon – the 7.7mm machine gun was deleted to save weight. Armour plate was installed for the first time behind the pilot's seat, along with a 37-gallon self-sealing fuel tank. Mitsubishi produced 93 examples of the 52c.

A6M6c MODEL 53c

The Sakae Model 31 A engine with water-methanol injection was fitted, but it proved unreliable and performance suffered as a result. Mitsubishi produced only one 53c.

A6M7 MODEL 63

This was the fighter/dive-bomber variant of the Zero-sen. Armament was the same as for the 52c, and in place of the normal centreline drop tank Mitsubishi developed a bomb rack that was capable of carrying a 500lb bomb. Two wing-mounted 33 imperial gallon (150-litre) drop tanks were provided in place of the centreline 72 imperial gallon (330-litre) drop tank.

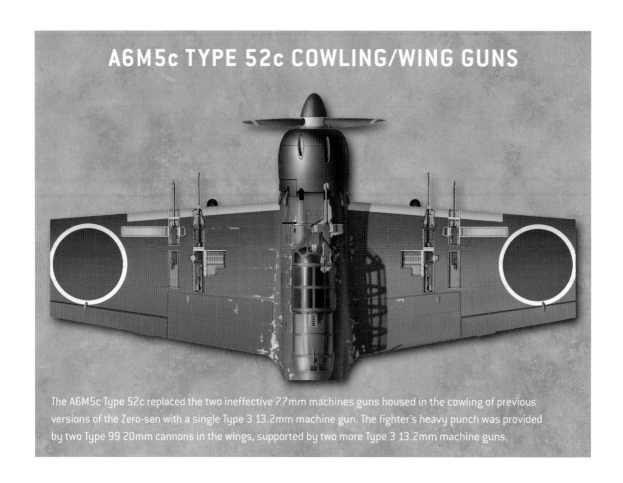

A6M5c TYPE 52c COWLING/WING GUNS

The A6M5c Type 52c replaced the two ineffective 7.7mm machines guns housed in the cowling of previous versions of the Zero-sen with a single Type 3 13.2mm machine gun. The fighter's heavy punch was provided by two Type 99 20mm cannons in the wings, supported by two more Type 3 13.2mm machine guns.

A6M8c MODEL 54c

For only the second time in the war, the Zero-sen was fitted with a more powerful engine in the form of Mitsubishi's Kinsei 62, developing 1,340hp. The bigger diameter Kinsei required a re-design of the forward fuselage that resulted in the fuselage-mounted machine gun being eliminated. The centreline bomb rack and wing-mounted drop tanks were retained. Maximum speed was 356mph at 19,685ft. Test pilots agreed it was the best model of the Zero-sen yet produced, and the fastest of them all. Only two were built.

A VIEW FROM THE COCKPIT

Very little was known about the Zero-sen in the early stages of the war, and it was not until July 1942 that the US managed to obtain a complete airframe (an A6M2 that had force-landed in the Aleutians the previous month) that could be test flown. On 4 September 1942, the Headquarters, US Army Air Forces Director of Intelligence Service issued Informational Intelligence Summary No 59:

The Japanese Zero Fighter
For sometime past, incomplete, confusing and occasionally conflicting information has

The main instrument panel removed from a captured Zero-sen Model 52. The instruments on top, from left to right, are the artificial horizon and turn and bank indicator. The second row consists of the exhaust temperature gauge, airspeed indicator, rate of climb indicator, combined fuel and oil pressure gauge and tachometer. The third row features the radio direction indicator, magneto switch, altimeter, manifold pressure gauge, oil temperature gauge and cylinder head temperature gauge. Dominating the centre of the instrument panel is the magnetic compass. (National Archives)

prevailed regarding the Japanese Zero Fighter. During recent weeks, examinations and investigations of crashed Zeros in various parts of the world have clarified the situation. For this reason, it is believed that the following detailed summary will prove of interest.

Cockpit

Although perhaps somewhat smaller than average, the cockpit provides ample room for a pilot of normal size. Instruments are conveniently arranged and visibility is good. No automatic flight control apparatus is installed, but the instrument panel contains practically all other flight and navigational instruments found in modern fighters, including artificial horizon, radio compass dial and bank-and-turn indicator. A rudder bar is provided rather than individual rudder pedals. Metal stirrup loops in hinged toe plates mounted at each end of the bar provide individual brake control, which is obtained through built-in Bowden wire connections to two hydraulic cylinders mounted on the cockpit floor just in front of the rudder bar. The entire rudder bar and fittings are manually adjustable fore and aft by means of a screw to accommodate pilots of different leg length.

The control stick is of normal design, but contains neither trigger nor gun selector switches. These are found upon the throttle handle on the left side of the cockpit. A small rocking-thumb lever in the top of the throttle selects in the forward position the 7.7mm nose guns and in the rearward position both the 7.7s and the 20mm wing guns. A long, curved trigger is fitted to the forward side of the throttle handle.

On the next inner quadrant, slightly below the throttle, a supercharger control lever is mounted. Inboard and slightly below the supercharger handle is the handle for the propeller pitch control. The mixture control handle is mounted on a separate quadrant, slightly higher and forward of the other group.

The air speed indicator is calibrated in knots and reads through a double scale from 40 to 160 and from 160 to 300 knots, equivalent to a range of 46 to 345 statute miles per hour. The altimeter is of somewhat unusual calibration and reads from 0 to 8 through a double circular scale with a single hand indicator. The unit of measurement, although not as yet definitely determined, is presumably kilometres.

How did the Seafire match up against the A6M5 Zero-sen? In October 1944, flight trials between a Seafire L IIC and a captured A6M5 Model 52 took place at the US Naval Air Station at Patuxent River, in Maryland. A subsequent report detailing the results of the trials read as follows:

Maximum Speed
The Seafire L IIC was faster below about 17,000ft, and the Zeke 52 was faster above that altitude.
At sea level the Seafire L IIC was 24mph faster than the Zeke 52.
At 5,000ft the Seafire L IIC was 24mph faster than the Zeke 52.
At 10,000ft the Seafire L IIC was 18mph faster than the Zeke 52.

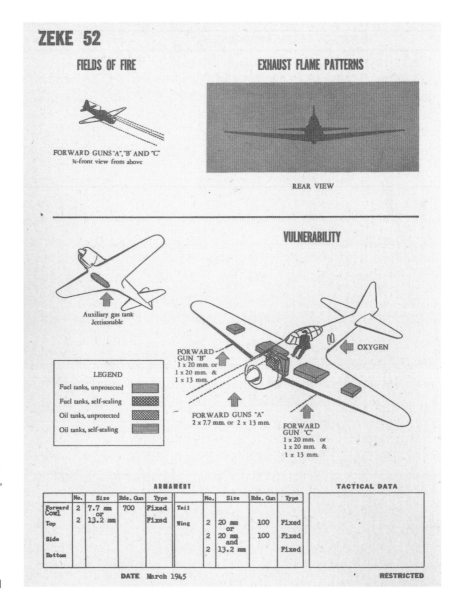

The Technical Air Intelligence Unit was the primary evaluation organisation concerned with flying captured Japanese aircraft, and it produced numerous briefing pamphlets such as this one for frontline units. The most studied aircraft was, of course, the Zero-sen. By March 1945 the Allies had learned everything they needed to know about the A6M, but at the beginning of the war it was quite the opposite. (Author's collection)

At 15,000ft the Seafire L IIC was 8mph faster than the Zeke 52.

At 20,000 feet the Seafire L IIC was 5mph slower than the Zeke 52.

At 25,000ft the Seafire L IIC was 10mph slower than the Zeke 52.

Top speeds attained were 338mph at 5,500ft for the Seafire and 335mph at 18,000ft for the Zeke 52.

Climb

The Zeke 52 climbs at a very steep angle, and gives an impression of a very high rate of climb. The Seafire L IIC, however, has a much better initial climb, and remains slightly superior up to 25,000ft. The climb of the Seafire is at a faster speed, but at a more shallow angle. The best climbing speeds for the Seafire and Zeke 52 were 160mph and 123mph respectively.

Dive

The Seafire is superior in the dive, although initial acceleration is similar. The 'Zeke' is a most unpleasant aircraft in a dive due to heavy stick forces and excessive vibration.

Turning Circle

The 'Zeke' can turn inside the Seafire L IIC at all heights.

Rate of Roll

The rate of roll of the two aircraft is similar at speeds below 180mph indicated, but above that the aileron stick forces of the 'Zeke' increase tremendously, and the Seafire becomes progressively superior.

Conclusions

Never dogfight with a 'Zeke 52' – it is too manoeuvrable. At low altitudes where the Seafire is at its best, it should make use of its superior rate of climb and speed to obtain a height advantage before attacking. If jumped, the Seafire should evade by using its superior rate of roll. The 'Zeke' cannot follow high-speed rolls and aileron turns. The Seafire L III, with the Merlin 55M, performed better than the L Mk IIC at all heights. At 6,000ft the L Mk III was capable of 358mph, making it the fastest of all the Merlin-engined Seafires.

All Allied fighter pilots were severely warned against dogfighting the Zero-sen. While the A6M could roll, turn and climb inside faster than any Allied fighter, that was not the whole story. The A6M5 was a slow-speed fighter. Its preferred speed was just 180mph or less, causing many Allied pilots to fight on its terms. The only Allied fighter that could out climb the A6M5 was the Seafire, this fact alone depriving the Zero-sen pilot of one of his major advantages. By climbing and diving, the Seafire would use its strengths to its advantage, and if the Zero-sen tried to emulate the Seafire, it could only do so by increasing its speed, which reduced its manoeuvrability to that of the Seafire. The latter's considerable edge in level speed and rate of climb at low and medium levels gave it the ability to disengage combat at will.

Amongst the pilots to use these attributes in combat in the final months of the war was Lt Gerry Murphy of 887 NAS, who claimed two victories in the Seafire's final aerial action of World War II:

When I first flew the Seafire it was pure exhilaration. Having flown the standard training aircraft, which didn't have anything approaching the speed and response, it was great in a climb and when turning, and you felt really in control. It was extremely responsive. I also flew the Hellcat, which was a very robust aircraft, but it was like flying a steamroller compared to the Seafire. It was big and heavy, but a great warhorse, and it could take an awful lot of punishment. Compared to the Hellcat, the Seafire was rather delicate. The Hellcat didn't have the response of the Seafire. It was the difference between a racehorse and a carthorse. The Seafire III was about 16 knots faster than the Hellcat and Corsair at low and medium altitudes.

Seafire L III and A6M5c Model 52c Comparison Specifications

	Seafire L III	A6M5c Model 52
Powerplant	1,585hp Merlin 55M	1,100hp Sakae Model 21
Dimensions		
Span	36ft 10in	36ft 1in
Length	30ft 2.5in	29ft 11in
Height	8ft (over cowling)	11ft 6in
Wing area	242 sq. ft	229.27 sq. ft
Weights		
Empty	6,204lb	4,136lb
Loaded	7,104lb	6,025lb
Performance		
Max speed	358mph at 6,000ft	348mph at 19,685ft
Range	400 miles (with drop tank)	657 miles
Climb	to 15,000ft in 5 min 30 sec	to 16,405ft in 5 min 50sec
Useful Ceiling	24,000ft	36,255ft
Armament:	2 x 20mm Hispano Cannon 4 x 0.303-in Brownings	2 x 20mm Type 99s 3 x 13.2mm Type 3s

THE STRATEGIC SITUATION

HMS *Indefatigable* heads through the Suez Canal on its way to the Pacific in late 1944. The Seafires of 894 NAS are still wearing the standard roundels for the European theatre. Prior to moving to the Pacific, *Indefatigable* was involved in Operation *Mascot*, which saw its air wing attack the German battleship *Tirpitz* – Seafire units 887 and 894 NASs provided CAPs and fighter sweeps. (ww2images.com)

The British Pacific Fleet, formed in November 1944, was designed to fight alongside the Americans in the Central Pacific. It was a formidable force centred on three fleet carriers – HMS *Illustrious*, *Victorious* and *Indomitable*, which were subsequently joined by *Formidable*, *Indefatigable* and *Implacable*. This would be the largest deployment of Royal Navy fleet carriers and aircraft during the war.

The units embarked in these vessels formed the 1st Aircraft Carrier Squadron (ACS), which consisted of 215 aircraft (later 255). The fighter component numbered 40 Seafires of No 24 Naval Fighter Wing (887 and 894 NASs), along with 12 Fireflies, 38 Hellcats and 73 Corsairs – the Seafires represented 27 percent of the total Fleet Air Arm fighter strength in the Pacific. The bulk of the fleet fighter defence was to be performed by the Seafire, leaving escort missions and fighter sweeps to be undertaken by 'longer-legged' Hellcats and Corsairs.

Typically, the carriers would conduct two days of strikes followed by two days of replenishment. From first light to dusk, the Seafires of No 24 Naval Fighter Wing would be required to fly 50 to 60 Combat Air Patrol (CAP) sorties. The F Mk IIIs would fly medium-level CAPs below a Corsair or Hellcat HiCAP and the L Mk IIIs would provide the low-level component close to the fleet.

Performing these missions was an incredible responsibility for the pilots involved when one considers the new threat posed to the fleet by the kamikaze, and their fanatical ability to hit, sink or damage surface vessels. In many ways the kamikaze threat was tailor made for the Seafire III, as its low-level performance and acceleration made it the premier interceptor against sea-skimming Japanese attacks.

While the Royal Navy and Fleet Air Arm had made great strides in providing the men and materiel for the war in the Pacific, No 24 Naval Fighter Wing was in a precarious position. Basic spare parts like propellers, undercarriage oleos and gunsights were in short supply in the Far East, and replacement Seafire IIIs were few and far between. There was also a serious shortage of experienced pilots. While the wing's leadership was of high quality, the majority of its pilots had little deck-landing experience and even less combat time.

When the fleet left Sydney harbour on 10 March 1945 for combat operations, there were only 37 Seafire pilots aboard HMS *Indefatigable* – 13 under the established complement. To deal with the low-level kamikaze threat, the number of Seafire L IIIs had been increased from 16 to 22 aircraft in 894 NAS, while the number of F Mk IIIs in 887 NAS was dropped from 24 to 18.

The British Pacific Fleet was now given the designation of Task Force 57, and on 25 March 1945 it would join with American Task Force 58 and 52.1 for Operation *Iceberg*, the invasion of Okinawa. *Iceberg* enjoyed the heaviest support for any open-sea amphibious operation of the war. Task Force 58 comprised 16 attack and light carriers, embarking more than 1,200 aircraft between them. The units to which the latter aircraft were assigned had the job of securing the northern approaches to Okinawa, as well as providing offensive and defensive support. Task Force 52.1, with its 15 CVEs (light carriers), undertook the close air support for the ground troops and provided local air defence. Task Force 57, with four carriers, two battleships, four cruisers, 11 destroyers and 231 aircraft, was the smallest of the task forces. To help support the invasion of Okinawa, the Royal Navy had been given the necessary, if thankless, task of flank protection.

The Sakishima Gunto archipelago was strategically placed between Formosa and Okinawa. The Imperial Japanese Navy still had many experienced units on Formosa, along with reinforcements on mainland China. The Royal Navy was tasked with

Reinforcing Japanese aircraft

KYUSHU

●Kagoshima

East China Sea

CHINA

Amami

Attacks by US fleet

Tokunoshima

Attacks by US fleet

Okinawa

●Taipai

Miyako

Yaeyama

Ishigaki

Attacks by Task Force 57

FORMOSA

0   150 miles
0   200 km

In late March 1945, the British Pacific Fleet, operating as Task Force 57, was given the job of neutralising Japanese airfields in the Sakishima Gunto archipelago, thus preventing aircraft kamikaze movements between Formosa and Okinawa.

neutralising the airfields in the Sakishima Gunto archipelago, thus preventing the movement of aircraft between Formosa and Okinawa.

On 26 March, all 40 Seafires of No 24 Naval Fighter Wing were ready for action. The first day of the operation went well for the Seafire units involved, with 72 sorties launched – 32 on medium-level CAPs and 40 on new 'Jack Patrols'. The latter was an American innovation designed as a last-ditch counter to the kamikazes that approached at sea level. The Seafire L III was the best fighter for this particular job. Held at less than 3,000ft, the patrols were controlled by visual fighter directors using a common local air defence R/T frequency.

After 12 days of strikes and numerous kamikaze attacks – *Indefatigable* was hit once – Task Force 57 had contributed 2,886 sorties, of which 450 were flown by aircraft from No 24 Naval Fighter Wing for an average of 36 sorties per strike day. The victory tallies for the Seafire pilots were slim, but they did shoot down three A6M Zero-sens and possibly damaged a Ki-61 'Tony'. The Seafire was now proven against the Zero-sen. With the experience gained, the pilots of No 24 Naval Fighter Wing would see even more action during *Iceberg II*.

By the time the invasion of Okinawa took place, the IJNAF and JAAF had virtually ceased to exist. The battles of attrition that had taken place in 1942–43 in the Southwest Pacific and New Guinea had gutted both air arms of pilots and aircraft. Most of the war's early veterans were now gone, and as their replacements had little experience their combat effectiveness was negligible. In the battle for the Marianas islands in June 1944, for example, the IJNAF would suffer one of its greatest defeats of the war.

In what has been recorded as the 'Great Marianas Turkey Shoot', the Japanese were able to field a force of nine aircraft carriers and 440 aircraft. The US Navy countered with

An A6M5 being refuelled. This crude and somewhat ineffective refuelling system was symptomatic of the Japanese inability to appreciate the basic needs required to field and equip an effective fighter force. Gasoline trucks were almost non-existent, and most units refuelled their aircraft using 200-gallon drums and a hand pump. (National Archives)

18 carriers and 475 Hellcats. When the smoke finally cleared, the Japanese had lost three carriers, with two others seriously damaged, and more than 300 aircraft (mostly Zero-sens) and pilots.

By the time of the Okinawa invasion the remnants of the IJN's heavy surface fleet were stranded in port due to a lack of fuel, aircraft and personnel. All remaining air groups were now ground-based, with the vast majority equipped with late mark versions of the Zero-sen. For the Japanese, the war situation was hopeless, and this is when they turned to the kamikaze. Whole fighter units were converted to the new role, and the aircraft most widely used was the battle-tested A6M.

After a short spell to rest and replenish, Task Force 57 was soon back in action as part of Operation *Iceberg II*. From 4 to 25 May, Task Force 57 once again flew strikes against the airfields in the Sakishima Gunto archipelago. The return to operations allowed No 24 Naval Fighter Wing to improve its score, and of the 11 Japanese fighters destroyed by Fleet Air Arm fighters during this period, five were credited to Seafires. Although this was a minuscule number when compared to US Navy claims

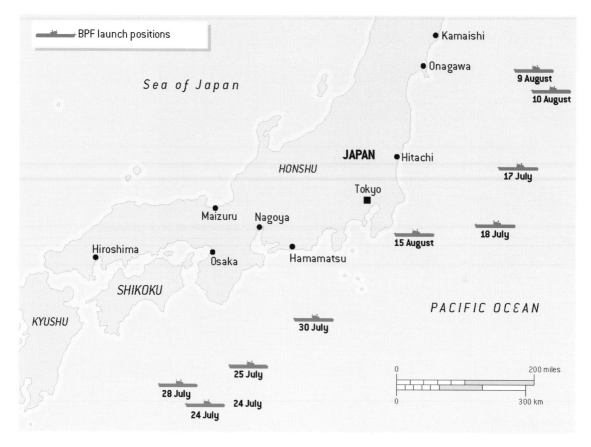

BPF launch positions

Kamaishi

Onagawa

Sea of Japan

9 August

10 August

JAPAN • Hitachi

HONSHU

17 July

Tokyo

Maizuru   Nagoya

18 July

15 August

Hiroshima   Osaka   Hamamatsu

SHIKOKU

30 July

PACIFIC OCEAN

KYUSHU

25 July

0   200 miles

28 July

24 July   0   300 km

24 July

The four aircraft carriers of the British Pacific Fleet's Task Force 37 launched a series of 'Ramrod' attacks on various targets in the Japanese home islands from 17 July through to 15 August 1945.

during *Iceberg II*, one has to remember that the British carriers had only seen 16 days of operations in 1945 up to 4 May. It must also be remembered that the Seafire was tied to a defensive role – they had to wait for the enemy to come to them. No 24 Naval Fighter Wing also improved its deck-landing record, as only nine aircraft were written off during the course of 578 sorties.

On 25 May Task Force 57 withdrew from the operational area and headed for Sydney, Australia. There, it was joined by HMS *Implacable* and the Seafires of 801 and 880 NASs, assigned to No 38 Naval Fighter Wing. Their addition brought the fleet's overall strength to 88 Seafire IIIs.

While ashore, attention was turned to the Seafire's endurance problem. No 24 Naval Fighter Wing opted for the standard Spitfire pattern 90 imperial gallon slipper tank, examples of which were obtained from the Royal Australian Air Force (RAAF). No 38 Naval Fighter Wing took a different approach to solving the range issue, however. After some experimentation, the P-40's 89 imperial gallon drop tank was selected. Sufficient stocks were made available (paid for with two crates of Johnny Walker scotch) from a USAAF Warhawk unit in New Guinea, and using a modified bomb rack, all 48 of the wing's aircraft were modified.

Following just three weeks of refit and repair, all preparations were made for the next round of strikes that would see the British Pacific Fleet directly targeting the Japanese home islands.

THE COMBATANTS

In January 1945 the Fleet Air Arm and the IJNAF were two vastly different forces. One was reaching the peak of its efficiency and combat strength, whilst the other was desperately short of fuel, aircraft and well-trained aircrew. In many ways, the years of conflict during World War II had seen a reversal of roles for the British and Japanese naval air arms.

At the beginning of the war, the Fleet Air Arm was comprised of a motley collection of obsolete biplanes and monoplanes, while the IJN had the world's foremost carrier striking force. Early victories in December 1941 shocked the world, and proved that the Japanese were masters in the art of carrier warfare. However, by January 1945 the Fleet Air Arm was a transformed force. Equipped with modern carriers and American Hellcats, Corsairs, Avengers and British-built Seafires and Fireflies, the Fleet Air Arm began striking at Japanese targets in Sumatra and the Bay of Bengal. In November 1944 the British Pacific Fleet was formed around the carriers HMS *Illustrious*, *Victorious* and *Indomitable*.

For the Japanese, the war had become a savage battle for survival by the autumn of 1944. Mostly equipped with the now obsolete A6M Zero-sen, the IJNAF had introduced a new weapon, the kamikaze. For all intents and purposes a force of little consequence, the IJNAF consisted of units that were manned in the main by pilots with only moderate levels of training. Incapable of taking on the vast Allied fleet sent to invade Okinawa through conventional means, novice naval aviators were turned into suicide bombers, while the more experienced pilots (who were few in number and exhausted from years of constant combat) navigated them to their targets, providing the kamikazes with a modicum of fighter protection along the way.

By 1945 the British Commonwealth Air Training Plan and the American output of pilots and aircrew had reached such a high level that they actually had a surplus of men

In this dramatic shot, an 801 NAS Seafire III loses a propeller blade crashing into *Implacable*'s barrier. The shock loading on the engine and its bearers in such an accident could cause severe damage, requiring extensive maintenance. This put a great strain on the already short-handed Seafire maintenance teams aboard both *Implacable* and *Indefatigable*. (Fleet Air Arm Museum)

ready to fly combat aircraft in the frontline. But even with this amazing output, Seafire pilot strength for both Nos 24 and 38 Naval Fighter Wings remained just at or below strength. In the early summer of 1945, the RAAF found itself with a large number of fighter pilots surplus to requirements. Many of these men had extensive operational experience in the Spitfire. Aware of the Fleet Air Arm's difficulties, the RAAF offered the services of 24 pilots, but the end of hostilities prevented them from seeing any combat.

FLEET AIR ARM TRAINING

By the final year of the war, a Fleet Air Arm trainee pilot could be found in one of two training systems. One was based in Great Britain and the other was in the United States, run by the US Navy under what was known as the 'Towers Scheme'. The latter was initially designed to train 30 pilots per month for the Fleet Air Arm and 100, mainly flying-boat crews, for the RAF.

In wartime Britain, everyone had to register for National Service, and for those who were keen on flying, most did not leave it to chance to express their interest in serving with the RAF. However, many who tried to enrol in the latter service, particularly after its widely publicised success in the Battle of Britain, were turned away because it had more volunteer pilots than it knew what to do with at the time. This was exactly what happened to future ace (and CO of 880 NAS in 1945) Lt Cdr Mike Crosley, who signed up to join the RAF in 1940, only to be told that it was effectively 'full'! Eager to get into the fight, he (and hundreds like him) was immediately accepted into the Fleet Air Arm to begin his training.

The first step in the long journey to becoming a Fleet Air Arm fighter pilot began at HMS *St Vincent*, at Gosport. Here, the new recruits were given a medical, followed

by an interview, during which the new recruit was asked if he wanted to be a pilot or observer. Once he had passed through this process, the new recruit would be sent home to await orders.

For naval aviators in Britain, wartime training started with a return to HMS *St Vincent*, where recruits joined in batches of 50 to 60 every four weeks. Each naval airman was kitted out with standard naval ratings' uniform, and they were classified as Naval Airmen 2nd Class. Recruits spent up to seven weeks at *St Vincent* marching, saluting, looking after their kit and learning how to handle a machine gun, as well as being taught basic navigation, Morse, semaphore and meteorology. At the end of 'basic' an examination had to be passed before elementary flying training could begin.

Initially, elementary flight training was handled by the RAF at Elmdon, now Birmingham International Airport, or Luton, now London Luton Airport. As training ramped up, additional facilities came on stream, with bases constructed throughout the Commonwealth that were made available through the British Commonwealth Air Training Plan. Training also took place at Naval Air Station (NAS) Pensacola, Florida.

After graduating from St Vincent as a leading naval airman, the new recruit could go one of two ways – to Elmdon or Luton, or on a troopship to Canada or Pensacola. For those sent to an RAF station in the UK, basic training or Elementary Flight Training (EFTS) would begin on the Miles Magister or de Havilland Tiger Moth.

It was during EFTS that the young student pilot came face to face with the mysteries of heavier-than-air flight. On the ground, the theory of flight made sense, but once in the air this frequently vanished, and the young pilot soon found himself battling a new force – panic. Squeezed into a tiny cockpit in small and fragile aircraft, the young pilot had to master his fear and take control of his machine. Many did not, and on average one in four washed out during elementary training.

SEAFIRE L III
COCKPIT

1. GGS Mk II Gyro gunsight
2. Flaps control
3. Engine speed indicator
4. Oxygen regulator
5. Oxygen regulator
6. Airspeed indictor
7. Artificial horizon
8. Rate of climb indicator
9. Stowage for reflector gunsight lamp
10. Radio controller
11. Clock
12. Landing gear indicator
13. Altimeter
14. Gun and cannon three-position push button
15. Turning indicator
16. Oil pressure gauge
17. Fuel pressure warning lamp
18. Boost pressure gauge
19. Oil temperature gauge
20. Radiator temperature gauge
21. Fuel contents gauge
22. Slow running cut out control
23. Signalling switchbox
24. Camera indicator supply plug
25. Instrument panel light
26. Ignition switch
27. Brake triple pressure gauge
28. Elevator tabs position indicator
29. Compass
30. Control column
31. Priming pump
32. Fuel tank pressurising cock control
33. R.1147 Remote control wave tuner
34. Throttle, mixture, propeller control
35. Rudder pedal
36. Undercarriage control lever
37. T.R. 1196 morsing key
38. Elevator trimming tab hand wheel
39. Air intake control
40. Radiator flap control lever
41. R. 1147/RT switch
42. Door hatch
43. Jettisonable control unit lever
44. IFF controls
45. Harness release
46. R. 1147 controller
47. Pressure head heater on/off switch
48. Seat
49. Undercarriage emergency lowering control
50. Map case
51. Oil dilution pushbutton
52. Oxygen supply cock
53. Arrestor hook lamp
54. Rudder trim wheel
55. Navigation lights switch

After three months of flying, the new pilot could have expected to have logged approximately 78 hours in the air. The next step was to the RAF's No 1 Service Flying Training School (SFTS) at Netheravon, where student pilots were streamed to fly either fighters or bombers. SFTS also meant bigger, more powerful aircraft such as the North American Harvard (SNJ-3 in US Navy service). Early on in the war, new students would have cut their teeth on old Hawker Hart biplanes and Fairey Battle monoplanes, as well as Harvards. The latter aircraft, compared to the Miles Magister or Tiger Moth, was a major step up. With a fully enclosed cockpit, it presented the student with a sea of instruments all powered by a big Pratt & Whitney engine. If the young pilot could handle the Harvard, he could then progress to a high performance fighter.

SFTS was where pilots learned formation flying, as well as aerobatics, navigation, instrument flying and fighter tactics. After three-and-half months of classes and flying, the new student would have approximately 120 hours' of flying time, including 20 hours at night. It was at this stage in their training that the new pilots were given their wings and commissioned into the Royal Navy Volunteer Reserve.

After a week of leave, newly minted pilots would return to the Royal Navy for their operational training. While the RAF had operational training units, the Fleet Air Arm had naval squadrons with numbers in the 700 series. Units like 761 NAS were designated as the advanced training squadrons of the Fleet Fighter School. By June 1944, 68 Seafires were being used for deck-landing training – a number of Miles Master IIs were also on strength.

Based at Yeovilton from its formation on 1 August 1941 and then Henstridge from 10 April 1943, 761 NAS was where new pilots learned to fly fighters. Early in the war they would have flown Sea Gladiators, Fulmars and Sea Hurricanes, but by 1944 the aircraft in the frontline were more advanced – Hellcats, Corsairs, Fireflies and Seafires.

Avengers of 828 NAS, Fireflies of 1771 NAS and Seafire IIIs of 880 NAS are lined up on deck as HMS *Implacable* turns into wind prior to launching a strike against Japanese bases on Truk atoll in June 1945. The long range slipper tanks newly fitted to the Seafires allowed them to participate in strikes, and freed them from their usual CAP assignments overhead the BPF. (Australian War Memorial Negative Number 019037)

A Seafire of No 38 Naval Fighter Wing is warmed up on board *Implacable* in mid 1945. The P-40 drop tank installation can be clearly seen. The latter adaptation was very successful, and proved more reliable than the standard 90-gallon slipper tank used by No 24 Naval Fighter Wing. No 38 Naval Fighter Wing obtained its drop tanks through a trade with the USAAF – the going rate was two crates of Johnny Walker scotch for 60 tanks. The Seafire's short range limited its usefulness for more than two years in the frontline. Why it took so long to hang a suitable drop tank onto the Spitfire/Seafire family is one of the war's great mysteries. If they had been available when the Seafire first entered service in late 1942, its contribution would have been greater, and its reputation may not have suffered as much. (Australian War Memorial Negative Number 019029)

It was also during this period of advanced training that the young students would make their first launches and landings from a carrier deck. Before a student was allowed near a carrier, he had to perform a number of Aerodrome Dummy Deck Landings on the airfield. The runway had white lines painted across it to represent make-believe arrestor hook wires. Directed by a 'batsman' or landing signal officer, the young pilot would be guided down to the runway, and hopefully to a successful landing. Once this was achieved the next step was to test his skills on a moving carrier. After six or more successful launches and landings, the new fighter pilot was ready for a squadron posting.

If assigned to train in the United States, the new recruit would be bound for NAS Pensacola. Here, the student would follow a similar training syllabus, with pre-flight, primary, intermediate and advanced pilot training, as well as advanced carrier training. He would fly different aircraft from his contemporaries in the UK, however, including the Naval Aircraft Factory N3N, Stearman N2S, North American NJ-1, SNJ Texan and Vultee SNV Valiant.

Clark Field, in the Philippines, was a staging base for the Allied drive on Japan. This unidentified Seafire III is either a replacement aircraft or one that was loaned to the Technical Air Intelligence Unit, Southwest Pacific Area, located at Clark Field. If indeed assigned to the latter outfit, it would have been used in comparative trials against captured Japanese fighter aircraft. (George J. Fleury via WW2Colour.com)

SEAFIRE CRASH ON H.M.S. "INDEFATIGABLE" PACIFIC. 1945.

On 16 April 1945 this 894 NAS Seafire L III jumped both of *Indefatigable's* barriers and crashed into a Firefly and Avenger, sending deck crew scrambling for safety. Unfortunately, many of the deck landing accidents suffered by the Seafire were due to pilot error. Low wind speeds over the deck caused a high approach, with the resulting hook-on-speeds being too excessive for the arrestor gear to cope with. Combined with the Seafire's poorly positioned hook and weak structure, this often proved disastrous. (Phil Jarrett)

The training offered in the US came with many advantages. Firstly, there was no fear of enemy attack, and secondly, excellent flying weather and higher performance aircraft, plus the accommodation and access to American amenities, made Pensacola a very pleasant place to be.

JAPANESE PILOT TRAINING

At the time of Pearl Harbor the IJNAF was an extremely well-trained force with a core of superbly trained carrier pilots. Many averaged 800 hours' flying time, and some had totals of up to 2,500 hours. At the beginning of the war, the IJNAF had between 3,000 and 4,000 pilots, of which around 1,500 were trained for carrier operations. The Eleventh Air Fleet that attacked Pearl Harbor boasted 600 pilots, each of which had an average of more than 600 hours' flying time.

By mid 1944, the inability of the Japanese to replace lost aviators resulted in a force that had just 50 percent of the average flying time of pilots flying in January 1942. In 1945 that average was down to less than 400 hours, with a minimum of 150. The Seafire pilots of the Fleet Air Arm would, therefore, find themselves fighting against three types of Japanese pilots – the kamikaze, the poorly trained new pilot and a handful of aces and experts.

Japan was an authoritarian regime with a rigid social structure and hierarchy. The methods employed to enlist and train aircrew were in many ways harsh and lengthy. The pool of healthy well-educated men eligible for flight training was far smaller than in the West. The cult of the big gun remained dominant in the IJN during the early part of the war, with naval officers expected to be seamen first. Carrier and air group commanders were not expected to be aviators. At the time of Pearl Harbor, only ten

A6M5c/7 ZERO-SEN COCKPIT

1. Type 98 reflector gunsight
2. Artificial horizon
3. Turn and bank indicator
4. Type 3 13.2mm machine gun
5. High-altitude automatic mixture control
6. Exhaust temperature gauge
7. Clock
8. Airspeed indicator
9. Magnetic compass
10. Rate of climb indicator
11. Fuel and oil pressure gauge
12. Tachometer
13. Emergency fuel pump lever

14. Direction finder control unit
15. Emergency power boost
16. Radio direction indicator
17. Magneto switch
18. Altimeter
19. Control column
20. Manifold pressure gauge
21. Oil temperature gauge
22. Cylinder head temperature gauge
23. Cockpit light
24. Throttle quadrant/20mm cannon firing lever
25. Primer

26. Oxygen supply gauge
27. Hydraulic pressure gauge
28. 20mm cannon master switch
29. Oil cooler shutter control
30. Cowl flap control
31. Radio control unit
32. Elevator trimming tab control
33. Circuit breakers
34. Rudder pedals
35. Wing tanks cooling air intake control
36. Emergency gear down lever
37. Loop antenna handle
38. Seat up/down lever

39. Fuel tank jettison handle
40. Fuselage tank fuel gauge
41. Wing tanks fuel gauge
42. Emergency fuel jettison lever
43. Fuselage /wing tanks switching cock
44. Wings tank selector lever
45. Bomb release lever
46. Seat
47. Arresting hook winding wheel
48. Wing tank fuel switching cock

Sitting high in the cockpit, a pilot taxis his A6M5 Type 52 fighter. Naval aviators would typically raise their seats when taxiing, thus giving them a better view forward when moving on the ground or recovering back aboard an aircraft carrier. While Seafire pilots could also adjust their seats, the view forward was almost completely obscured by the engine cowling and exhaust stubs. Because of this, the flightdeck could not be seen during the last 50 yards of the landing. (National Archives)

percent of all IJNAF pilots were officers and academy graduates of the Naval Academy at Eta Jima. Naval Academy graduates were not encouraged to enter aviation, and instead of integrating naval aviators like the US Navy did, the IJN segregated them.

In order to bolster the number of aviators, the Japanese set up the Flight Reserve Enlisted Training Programme in 1928. Physically and academically gifted teenagers between the ages of 15 and 17 were chosen, and all had to be primary school graduates – in 1937 the standard was raised to middle school. These young men would spend up to three years at sea prior to being sent to aviation training.

Like their brother aviators who had been recruited from the fleet, the reserve youths were enlisted men. Amazingly, 90 percent of Japanese naval pilots were either enlisted men or 'non-coms'. As the war progressed, the huge divide that separated the enlisted men from officers did nothing for morale in the field.

1941 saw a major expansion of the reserve pilot programme, but the results were not felt on the frontlines until 1943. Like the training methods in the West, the Japanese followed a similar programme, but their methods were harsh and very selective. Japanese ace Saburo Sakai recalled that only 75 men from a pool of 1,500 were accepted for flight training. The harsh training regime that followed was designed to create a warrior mentality.

In addition to ground and flight instruction, the new recruits were also subjected to a gruelling physical programme which included swimming, holding one's breath, standing on heads, wrestling, diving off a platform onto the ground, hanging with one hand from an iron bar and walking on your hands! If one performed poorly, the shame of expulsion was the result. How much of this physical training helped in the creation of a fighter pilot is open to debate, and as the war progressed the IJNAF dispensed with it.

After the war the US Navy studied the Japanese air training system and produced a detailed report, a portion of which follows:

Fuelled and armed, these A6M5cs warm up prior to taking off from an airfield somewhere in the Philippines in late 1944. The A6M5c Type 52 was the most heavily armed and armoured Zero-sen variant. While these improvements were made, engine power stayed the same, greatly hindering the fighter's performance. The aircraft did not match up well against both American and British carrier-borne fighters of the late-war period. (Phil Jarrett)

Training

1. The Bureau of Training, Kyoiku Kyoku, at Naval Air Headquarters lays down the lines for the training of all Naval Air Personnel. A single Combined Air Training Command, Rengo Koku Sotai, based at Gifu, is responsible for carrying out the policy thus laid down.

2. There are six Combined Air Groups (Rengo Kokutai), Nos 11–14 and 18 and 19, subordinate to this command in which all IJNAF personnel are trained. These combined Air Groups are Headquarter Staffs, the training itself being given in Training Air Groups (Kokutai), under the overall supervision of the Combined Air Group Headquarters.

3. Each Combined Air Group is responsible for training in a particular area. At the same time the training given by one Combined Air Group is not the same as that given by another. The following table show the location of each group, and the nature of the training it conducts: –

Command	Location	Function
Combined Air Group 11	Central Honshu	mainly elementary flying training
Combined Air Group 12	Kyushu	mainly advanced flying training
Combined Air Group 13	Japan/China	navigation, W/T air gunnery
Combined Air Group 14	Formosa	advanced flying training
Combined Air Group 18	Japan	unknown
Combined Air Group 19	Japan	unknown

4. Training Air Groups carrying out the training of flying and ground personnel number about 100 in total. Apart from six in Formosa, and isolated ones in the Philippines, Indo China, China and Korea, all these Air Groups are in Japan (unlike the JAAF, most of whose training units are overseas).

5. There are five types of Training Air Groups:

A) Preparatory

Pre-flight training air groups for potential aircrews. Recruits are drawn from the IJN, from civil life or from the Youth Air Training Corps (an organisation similar to the Air Training Corps in the RAF). At the end of this training, which varies in length according to the age of the recruit, trainees are classified into pilots, navigators, bomb-aimers, air-gunners and wireless operators.

B) Disciplinary

'Boot-training' groups for potential ground personnel

C) Specialist Training

Specialist training groups exist for providing courses of instruction for other than pilot aircrews graduating from (A) and (B).

D) Elementary Flying Training

The elementary flying training groups are fed by recruits from the groups under (A) who have graduated as potential pilots. These groups specialise in fighter, bomber or reconnaissance training for pilots graduating from the elementary flying training groups.

E) Operational Training

Operational flying training is carried out in operational units, to which pilots are posted after completing their advanced flying training. Often, these units are ones being newly formed in Japan. Operational training is supervised by the command to which the operational unit is subordinated. This, in most cases, is an Air Flotilla, which for training purposes is normally given the use of two or three airfields, one or two 'target' ships and, when required, a training aircraft carrier.

Pilots of the 203rd Kokutai's 303rd Hikotai study their day's assignment at Kagoshima Naval Air Station in May 1945. On the left is CPO Takeo Tanimizu (32 victories), whilst the pilot on the right has an 8mm Nambu pistol in his hand. (Takeo Tanimizu)

Expansion of JNAF Training System

As a result of the increasing demands of the war, considerable expansion in the training system took place in late 1943 and the spring of 1944. This expansion was of two kinds:

A. an increase in the number of training groups of all kinds

B. an increase in the numbers of aircraft used at many of the elementary and advanced Flying Training Groups.

The supply of personnel for the enlarged system was drawn mostly from university and higher school graduate classes, conscripted in 1943.

Individual Training of IJNAF Personnel

Pre-flight Training

The length of the pre-flight course for potential aircrew varies according to the age and educational background of the entrant. For volunteers straight from school, there is a course lasting for 1½–2½ years that is primarily educational and cultural in nature, but including instruction of an elementary kind in various aspects of IJNAF work. Recruits of military age take a six- or eight-week pre-flight course designed to improve their physique and introduce them generally to the IJNAF routine. An 'aptitude for flying' test is given at the end of both of these courses, after which recruits are divided into three classes, pilots, navigators and W/T operators, and posted to other Air Groups for further training. Pilots go onto elementary flying training Air Groups.

Elementary Flying Training

No distinction is made at this stage between fighter, bomber or reconnaissance pilots, all of whom train together on an elementary biplane trainer (most likely the Yokosuka K2Y2 Navy Type 3 basic trainer). The course lasts four months, instruction being given in

Sitting high in his cockpit, a kamikaze pilot taxis out in his bomb-laden A6M5 Zero-sen during Leyte operations in October–November 1944. The weapon strapped to his fighter is a Type 99 1650lb general-purpose bomb. In the hands of a skilled and determined pilot, this proved to be a deadly combination. (Naval Historical Center)

take-offs, landings and circuits. Flying time is about 100 hours, most of which are flown on aircraft with dual control. Classes are held in the principles of flying, with some instruction also in aircraft maintenance and meteorology. At the end of this course trainees are designated as fighter, bomber or reconnaissance pilots and posted to Air Groups specialising in these types.

Advanced Flying Training

Four months are spent at the Advanced Flying Training Air Groups. Advanced trainers and obsolescent operational aircraft are used, flying time being in the region of 100 hours for fighter pilots, including about ten on 'conversion' [aircraft used would include the Yokosuka K5Y1 biplane Navy Type 93 Intermediate Trainer, Mitsubishi A5M4 'Claude' Navy Type 96 monoplane fighter and, later in the war, Mitsubishi A6M2-K and A6M5-K two-seat advanced trainer versions of the Zero-sen]. Combat tactics, air-firing, navigation, etc., are taught, with more importance being attached to the pilot's actual performance in the air than to his theoretical knowledge. In the case of fighters, for example, no theoretical test at all is given.

Operational Training

Having completed the advanced flying course, pilots are posted to an operational unit for operational training. Operational training is intensive, considerable time being spent teaching formation flying, as well as combat tactics, carrier landings and night flying. The time spent on operational training varies from two to six months according to operational requirements, and, therefore, no definite figure can be given for flying hours. The minimum target is believed to be 60 hours.

Pilot training for both the JAAF and IJNAF was slow in providing well-trained pilots to replace combat losses. By 1945 the threat of invasion of the Japanese

War prizes bound for America aboard USS *Chopee* in late 1945. The Zero-sen closest to the camera is an A6M5b Type 52b model, identified by the longer gun port on the right side of the cowling. This was enlarged to accommodate the Type 3 13.2mm machine gun. Complete armament consisted of two 20mm cannon and single 7.7mm and one 13.2mm machine guns. (National Archives)

homeland was the primary concern of the JAAF and IJNAF. By the end of the war nearly 10,700 aircraft had been assigned the kamikaze role, and the 18,000 pilots available for combat had, on average, just 100 flying hours apiece. By March 1945 all flying training had been terminated.

Abandoned IJNAF aircraft littered Atsugi airfield in November 1945. In the foreground is an A6M5c Type 52c, its tail code identifying it as having belonged to the 302nd Kokutai. Dumped alongside this Zero-sen is one of its intended replacements, the J2M3 Raiden. The latter fighter's four-bladed propeller is still attached to its powerful 1,800hp Kasei 23a engine. (National Archives)

COMBAT

SEAFIRE TACTICS

The evolution of the aircraft carrier during World War II was extraordinary. For the Royal Navy, it was a complete transformation. British carrier doctrine pre-war was based on the Fleet Air Arm using its aircraft to shadow an enemy fleet and slowing it down with its torpedo-bombers. Once that was accomplished, battleships would provide the final blow. By 1945 the aircraft carrier, and its aircraft, could accomplish all that and more.

The aircraft carrier and the new 'carrier task forces' now gave naval commanders the ability to strike at the enemy directly. The British Pacific Fleet, equipped with American-built Hellcats, Corsairs and Avengers and British-built Fireflies and Seafires, had proven itself to be an effective offensive force. Now it would turn its attention to the Japanese home islands and the last Fleet Air Arm offensive of the war.

By the time the Seafire reached the Pacific theatre of war, Spitfire Mk VIIIs, Mk IXs and Griffon-engined Mk XIVs were dominating the skies over Europe. These variants were the most advanced versions of the legendary Vickers-Supermarine fighter to see combat in World War II, yet the Fleet Air Arm's Seafire III was, for all intents and purposes, a 1941 Spitfire V! The roles it was asked to perform were many and varied – interceptor, fighter escort, dive-bomber and reconnaissance – all from the deck of an aircraft carrier.

While the faults of the Seafire as a carrier aircraft were many, its performance as a combat aircraft was superb. In the Pacific, the Seafire would battle a new and unyielding foe – the kamikaze. For this role the Seafire was well equipped. Because of its exceptional performance at medium and low altitudes, the Seafire was assigned as a last-ditch interceptor. If the kamikazes made it through the higher-level Corsairs

An all-British affair – Fireflies (from 1772 NAS) and Seafires are ready to launch on another strike against Japanese targets from *Indefatigable*. The 894 NAS Seafires are equipped with 90-gallon slipper tanks. Designed for ferry purposes only, the slipper tank was not as reliable as the 89-gallon P-40 tank used by No 38 Naval Fighter Wing's Seafire units embarked in *Implacable*. The 90-gallon tanks gave the Seafire an escort and strike capability in the last few months of the war, and brought the fighter's range close to that achieved by American naval fighters of the late war period. (Fleet Air Arm Museum)

and Hellcats, it would be up to the Seafires to engage them at altitudes of less than 3,000ft within ten miles of the destroyer screen. Each CAP would consist of eight Seafires, equipped with 90-gallon slipper tanks. The latter would allow the fighters to remain airborne for three hours and ten minutes.

The first kamikaze Zero-sen confirmed shot down fell to the guns of Sub Lt Richard H. Reynolds. On 1 April 1945, four A6Ms, led by a radar-equipped search and attack aircraft, were intercepted by high-level Hellcats. One Zero-sen was shot down and three escaped into cloud, later to reappear over the British carriers. At 0725 hrs the battleship HMS *King George V* was strafed by one of the A6Ms. As it pulled out of its dive, the fighter was intercepted by Sub Lt Reynolds of 890 NAS. Although well within the Gun Defence Zone, the Seafire pilot pressed home his attack nevertheless. Scoring cannon strikes on the enemy fighter's port wing, Reynolds watched as the Zero-sen rolled over and dived into *Indefatigable*.

Twenty minutes later, Reynolds was able to despatch two more kamikaze Zero-sens to become the Fleet Air Arm's sole Seafire ace – he had shared in the destruction of two German Bv 138 flying-boats in the Arctic in August 1944.

Fellow ace Lt Cdr 'Mike' Crosley of 880 NAS, embarked in *Implacable*, had these thoughts regarding the kamikaze threat:

The kamikaze was a weird form of terrorism which seemed to us to deserve nothing but a painful death and eternal damnation. With their clever, decoy-led, low-level approach below the radar of the carrier air defence, it was worrying to think that 100 percent kills would be necessary before a sure defence could be provided. Each one of these part-trained, one-way aviators could park a 500lb bomb within a few feet of his aiming point if he was allowed to get within a few miles of the fleet. However, we felt that the Seafire, of all aircraft, would be the best possible defence in such circumstances, and we were not too frightened provided we could see the kamikazes coming.

In the ground attack dive-bombing role the Seafire was also effective. Here, Lt Cdr Crosley developed a method of attack that would greatly reduce losses due to flak. Instead of running into the target from line astern, one aircraft following the other, Crosley devised a method in which up to 16 Seafires would dive on it simultaneously from three different directions. Using this method, an attack could be completed within about 20 seconds, thus giving the enemy gunners a confusing array of targets, and little time to find their mark. This method also significantly reduced the time taken for the unit to re-form, thus saving valuable fuel.

On 14 June 1945, Seafires from No 38 Naval Fighter Wing, embarked in *Implacable*, dive-bombed the oil storage tanks on Dublon Island, at Truk Lagoon. No direct hits were recorded, but the near misses fissured the tanks.

The British carriers *Victorious*, *Formidable* and *Implacable* (designated Task Force 37) rendezvoused with American Task Force 38.2 500 miles north of Manus on 16 July 1945. *Indefatigable* would join them four days later. On 17 July Task Force 37 launched its first missions against Japan – the first by any British or Commonwealth

No 38 Naval Fighter Wing conducted air strikes against Truk Lagoon on 14–15 June 1945. N 151 of 801 NAS was damaged by flak and crash-landed aboard *Implacable*. Here, the pilot's door can be seen open. Naval aviators used a steady, left-hand turning approach all the way down to the deck when landing in a Seafire. With his canopy hood slid back, cockpit door down, goggles on and his head literally in the slipstream out the left side of the cockpit, the Seafire pilot was just able to see part of the flightdeck and batsman before recovering back aboard the carrier. Landing accidents accounted for 30 percent of all Seafire mishaps. (Fleet Air Arm)

On 4 May 1945 during
Operation *Iceberg II*, three
Seafire L IIIs of 894 NAS
intercepted a group of
kamikazes attempting to
attack the British Pacific Fleet.
The latter aircraft were part of
a force of 15 fighters that had
taken off from Giran, on
Formosa. Four of the A6Ms,
flying at just 500ft, were
sighted at 1730 hrs and
Lt Lieutenant A. S. Macleod
RNZNVR (Senior Pilot of 894
NAS) led his CAP in a head-on
attack and began firing at the
leading enemy aircraft. The
closing speed between the
two fighters was very high,
and, incredibly, Lt Macleod
expended only 20 rounds
per cannon and 15 rounds
per machine gun to down the
enemy aircraft that he had
been targeting. The Zero-sen
burst into flames and plunged
into the sea.

aircraft of the war. The Seafires of No 38 Naval Fighter Wing flew 'Ramrod' missions – a fighter sweep against targets of opportunity within briefed areas – as part of this strike. The wing attacked Kionoke, Naruto and Miyakawa airfields.

24 July was the high water mark for Task Force 37, with a total of 416 sorties being flown. Some 261 were against Japanese land and inshore targets, with the remaining 155 being defensive patrols, CAP and anti-submarine patrols. The Seafires from Nos 24 and 38 Naval Fighter Wings provided 76 of the offensive sorties – a very high number when one considers that they were also responsible for the fighter defence of the fleet.

Incredibly, 9 August (the second atomic bomb attack on Japan) would mark the supreme moment for the Fleet Air Arm's strike aircraft. Some 258 Avengers, Corsairs, Hellcats, Fireflies and Seafires found and attacked targets, delivering the greatest weight of ordnance dropped or fired on 'any enemy on any one day' by aircraft operating from British carriers during the whole war. More than 120 tons of bombs and cannon shells were expended. The attacks on the Japanese mainland ended on 10 August with 372 sorties flown. Task Force 37 withdrew the following day.

A6M ZERO-SEN TACTICS

Japanese 'fighter tactics' at this point in the war can best be described as desperate. Putting aside the kamikaze attacks, the tactics used by the IJNAF pilots were of little consequence, as good pilots and aircraft were too few in number to make any difference. Squadrons were forced to soldier on with the now completely obsolete A6M Zero-sen, and while it was still an effective opponent in skilled hands, the latter were being killed off rapidly.

Early in the war the Japanese adopted the three-aeroplane section known as the shotai as its standard tactical formation. It was similar to the British V formation, but was much more flexible. In the Japanese version, the flight leader flew well ahead of his two wingmen. While the leader held a steady course, his wingmen would weave from left to right and up and down. This protected the formation from surprise attack by covering many of the blind spots.

Once a target was found, instead of attacking as a single formation, the wingmen trailed the leader and attacked the target in succession. When several shotai were involved, the impact was devastating.

While effective in the attack mode, the shotai was a liability when attacked. Once broken up, the Japanese pilots would have to fight individually, hoping to use their superior manoeuvrability to deadly effect. The Zero-sen performed well below 20,000ft, and was at its best in a slow-turning combat of 200 knots or less. This system worked well for several years, but by 1944 the IJNAF had converted to the Allied four-aeroplane formation.

By 1945 the Japanese war effort was a lost cause. Defeats in the Philippines and on Iwo Jima had placed Allied forces right on the doorstep of Japan, and starting in February American carrier aircraft from Task Force 58 began to attack airfields in the Tokyo area. The air defence of Japan was now the top priority. Units like the 203rd Kokutai, having suffered heavy losses over the Philippines and Okinawa, were reformed. Although the 203rd Kokutai was led by an experienced veteran (Capt Ryutaro Yamanaka), the unit was comprised mostly of fresh flight school graduates flying the venerable Zero-sen. Added to the fact that most IJNAF fighter units were ordered to conserve fuel and fighters for one big kamikaze attack, few if any of the new graduates were able to obtain any combat experience.

KAMIKAZE TACTICS

The invasion of the Philippines by American forces and the humiliating defeat of VAdm Jisaburo Osawa's fleet at the battle of the Philippine Sea forced the IJNAF to adopt tactics of the most desperate nature. VAdm Takijiro Onishi, CO of the 1st Air Fleet, devised the radical idea of strapping a 250kg bomb to the Zero-sen and asking for volunteers to crash themselves onto American aircraft carriers. Newer versions of the A6M would provide escort, navigation and confirmation of the results.

With few aeroplanes and no fuel to train new pilots, most, if not all, of the IJNAF's naval aviators knew their situation was hopeless. This in turn led them to volunteer in droves. Success would soon follow on 25 October 1944 when bomb-carrying Zero-sens from the 201st Kokutai managed to sink the escort carrier USS *St Lo* and damage six other vessels.

A6Ms were used in the vast majority of kamikaze attacks simply because they were available in the greatest numbers, and their performance gave the pilots their best chance of surviving the screen of fighters and anti-aircraft fire.

The Japanese quickly realised that the radar coverage of a ship was not very good past 20 miles, so they adapted a 'zero feet' approach with a twist. Most of the suicide pilots were inexperienced naval aviators, and they needed an escort to guide them to their targets. At approximately 20 miles from the Allied fleet, the experienced naval aviators would pull up and expose themselves to radar, thus hopefully drawing away the high-flying Hellcat and Corsair CAPs and leaving the low-flying kamikazes to approach their targets unseen.

After March 1945, more than half of the Japanese pilots available sacrificed themselves in suicide attacks. These last-ditch tactics cost the IJNAF dearly, and as it did in the beginning of the war, the Zero-sen played a leading role in the campaign. Of the 2,363 IJNAF aeroplanes that took off on kamikaze flights, 1,189 were A6Ms

This blurred, but revealing, photograph graphically reveals what the young Seafire pilots were up against. The kamikaze was a new and frightening foe, and one that required a defence with a 100 percent kill ratio for any hope of success. This Zero-sen, carrying a 550lb bomb, was photographed diving on USS *Enterprise* in May 1945. (National Archives)

RICHARD HENRY REYNOLDS

Sub Lt Richard Reynolds of 894 NAS was the highest-scoring Seafire pilot of the war, and he had the honour of shooting down more kamikaze aircraft than any other naval aviator in the entire Fleet Air Arm. Richard Henry Reynolds was born on 12 October 1923 and went to school in Cambridge. He then joined the Royal Navy as a naval airman at HMS *St Vincent*, in Gosport. During the autumn of 1943 he underwent deck-landing training aboard the carrier HMS *Ravager* in the Firth of Clyde, and in March 1944 he was commissioned as a sub-lieutenant in the Royal Navy Volunteer Reserve. Shortly after Reynolds joined 894 NAS aboard *Indefatigable*.

On 29 August 1944 he would score his first aerial victories. During Operation *Goodwood* (a series of four Fleet Air Arm strikes against the German battleship *Tirpitz*, holed up in a Norwegian fjord), Sub Lt Reynolds and Lt H. T. Palmer sighted a German Bv 138C flying-boat shadowing the fleet. With a cloud base of just 700ft and visibility a mere half-mile, the Seafire pilots caught the German aircraft before could disappear. They made quick work of their prey, and within minutes another Bv 138C had also been downed. Reynolds was mentioned in despatches.

Later that year *Indefatigable* went out to the Far East to join the British Pacific Fleet. In January 1945, 894 NAS flew CAPs while the fleet carried out strikes against Sumatran oil refineries. Starting in April, *Indefatigable* and three other British carriers took part in Operation *Iceberg*.

At 0725 hrs on 1 April, a lone kamikaze pilot in a Zero-sen broke through the cloud and strafed the battleship HMS *King George V*. As it pulled out of its dive, Sub Lt Reynolds entered the Gun Defence Zone and gave chase. At long range, and with extreme deflection, Reynolds managed to score cannon hits along the enemy fighter's port wing-root, but it was not enough. Before he could reach a better firing position, the IJNAF pilot rolled the A6M onto its back and plunged into *Indefatigable*. Four officers and ten ratings were killed and 16 wounded. The armoured deck saved the carrier from further damage, and flying operations resumed less than an hour later.

Twenty minutes later, a second Zero-sen appeared and dropped a bomb, narrowly missing the destroyer HMS *Ulster*. Reynolds gave chase, and in two short firing passes despatched the intruder. Moments later, he sighted

(Via C F Shores via Andrew Thomas)

another A6M, and this one chose to stay and fight. The Japanese pilot tried to force Reynolds into a turning fight, but he kept up his speed and used the Seafire's superior climbing and diving performance to reach a favourable firing position. With his fifth, and final, burst he sent the A6M crashing into the Pacific. Sub Lt Reynolds would share in the destruction of another Zero-sen during Operation *Iceberg II* on 4 May. He was awarded a Distinguished Service Cross for his perfomance in both operations

Sub Lt Reynold's exceptional flying abilities saw him offered a regular Royal Navy commission in 1946. In 1948 he joined 806 NAS, flying the Hawker Sea Fury. He passed the Empire Test Pilots' Course and went to Boscombe Down as a test pilot. In 1952 Reynolds went back to sea aboard the carrier HMS *Eagle*, and flew Supermarine Attackers with 803 NAS. From March 1955 to May 1956 he commanded 811 NAS, flying the Hawker Sea Hawk. In 1957 he returned to HMS *Eagle* as ship's company, and after promotion to commander in December of that year, Reynolds had his first, and only, sea command, the destroyer HMS *Contest*. Commander (Air) aboard HMS *Ark Royal* from 1959 to 1961, Richard Reynolds retired from service in 1971 and passed away in 1999.

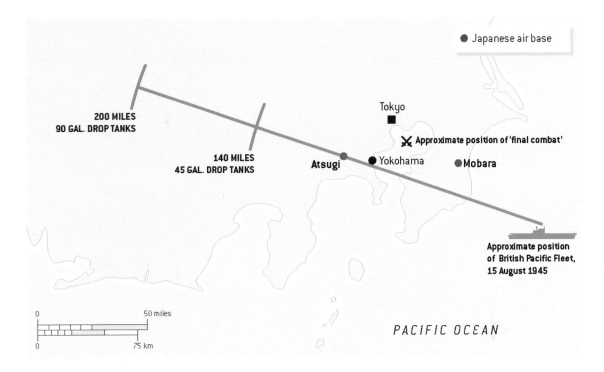

- ● Japanese air base

200 MILES
90 GAL. DROP TANKS

140 MILES
45 GAL. DROP TANKS

Tokyo

✖ Approximate position of 'final combat'

Atsugi ● ● Yokohama ● Mobara

Approximate position
of British Pacific Fleet,
15 August 1945

0   50 miles

0   75 km

PACIFIC OCEAN

fighters. Approximately 2,530 IJNAF pilots and aircrew lost their lives. In sharp contrast to those astounding numbers, Seafire pilots succeeded in downing just eight kamikaze Zero-sens.

During operations off Okinawa, the British carriers were hit seven times, but they were never put out of action. The survivability of the British 'flattops' when compared to their American cousins is legendary. All Royal Navy carriers were built with an armoured deck and hangers, this pre-war design trait being born out of necessity. Hobbled for funding by the RAF, the Fleet Air Arm was allocated few resources, in particular advanced fighters. Worried, therefore, about the potential lack of fighter cover, the Royal Navy wisely built their carriers to take damage, specifically from 6-in shells and 500lb bombs. The US Navy based its construction philosophy on the fact that its carriers would be well defended by embarked fighters.

Throughout World War II, British carriers proved themselves capable of taking direct hits either from bombs or, latterly, kamikazes. However, this protection came at a price. Because of their armour, the vessels carried fewer aircraft – the four British carriers between them had only 151 fighters, whereas one American *Essex* class carrier of comparable size was capable of operating 74. The Royal Navy carriers were also slower.

The Seafire was hamstrung for much of World War II by its poor range on internal fuel. However, by the time the British Pacific Fleet was committed to the final attacks on the Japanese home islands, its Seafire units had equipped their aircraft with either purpose built 90 Imp gal Spitfire slipper tanks or surplus P-40 89 Imp Gal drop tanks. As this map shows, these allowed the fighters to range deep inland.

LAST COMBAT

While the Allies waited for any signs of surrender from the Japanese, American Task Force 38 would remain off the coast of Japan. It was joined by a token Royal Navy group built around the carrier *Indefatigable* and the battleship *King George V*, designated Task Force 38.5.

A close up of the centreline drop tank fitted to late war Zero-sens. With the engine cowling gills open, the individual exhaust stacks can also be clearly seen. First incorporated in the A6M5 Type 52 variant, the ejector-type exhaust stacks directed high-velocity exhaust gas backward for additional thrust. The centreline drop tank carried 72.6 imperial gallons of fuel. This gave the A6M5 a maximum range of 1,037 nautical miles. (National Archives)

Between 13 and 15 August, *Indefatigable* continued to attack targets around the Tokyo area. With no signs of immediate surrender, strikes were ordered to commence again at dawn on the 15th. At 0400 hrs a Firefly 'Ramrod' was launched, followed by six Avengers with an escort of eight Seafires from 887 and 894 NASs. Five L Mk IIIs, led by Lt F. Hockley, would provide close and middle cover, while Sub Lt Vic Lowden led the top cover with the remaining three Seafire F IIIs. As the Avengers approached their designated target, Kisarazu airfield, they found it shrouded in cloud, forcing them to attack their alternate target – a chemical factory near Odaki Bay.

Despite the war being all but over, the IJNAF was still mounting air defence sorties and kamikaze attacks. One of the units involved was the 302nd Kokutai, based at Atsugi air base on the Kanto Plain southwest of Tokyo. Formed on 1 March 1944 and given the task of protecting the nation's capital against USAAF B-29 bombers, the 302nd had been credited with 300 victories by August 1945. The group initially boasted a mixed interceptor force comprising 48 fighters (A6M5c/7 Zero-sens and J2M3 Raidens) and 24 nightfighters (J1N2 Model 21 Gekkos).

There were very few veterans left in its ranks by the final weeks of the conflict, however, and most of its pilots had been transferred in from other branches such as seaplanes, flying-boats and carrier bombers. By May 1945, the 302nd Kokutai was down to just ten operational aircraft, most of which had been dispersed in anticipation of the final battle.

The 252nd Kokutai, based at Mobara airfield, east of Tokyo Bay, was also assigned the task of air defence. Like the 302nd, it too was equipped with a limited number of late model Zero-sens.

On the morning of 15 August, Allied carrier aircraft were detected heading for the Tokyo area. The 302nd commander, Capt Yasuna Kozono, ordered all serviceable fighters airborne. Led by Lt Yutaka Morioka (who was destined to become an ace that day), four J2M3 Raidens and eight A6M5c/A6M7 Zero-sens took to the air. The 252nd Kokutai also launched fighters, with Lt Cdr Moriyasu Hidaka leading a group of eight or nine Zero-sens towards a large formation of enemy aircraft.

The air space over Tokyo Bay and surrounding areas proved to be a crowded place on the 15th. Along with the aircraft from *Indefatigable*, there were six F6F-5 Hellcats from VF-88 and an unknown number of FG-1 Corsairs from VBF-88 (both from Carrier Air Group 88, embarked in USS *Yorktown* (CV-10)) heading for the IJNAF airfields at Atsugi and Hokoda.

It has recently been claimed that the Japanese fighters encountered by the Fleet Air Arm that morning were almost certainly from the 302nd Kokutai, led by Lt Morioka. This does not mesh with Lt Morioka's claim for a single Hellcat shot down that day, however. His original orders were to head to Kisarazu airfield, and once overhead the base, he found a hangar on fire, smoking violently. Could the earlier Firefly 'Ramrod' launched ahead of the Avengers and Seafires have reached Kisarazu airfield and attacked it before the weather closed in? According to Lt Morioka, his

Pilots of the 2nd Hikotai of the 302nd Kokutai pose for the camera at Atsugi in late 1944. Fighter pilots on both sides shared many things in common, but the one that stood out the most was their young age. Here, these young grim-faced pilots face the camera knowing that their chances of survival were extremely slim. Sat in the centre of the front row is the hikotai CO, Lt Yutaka Morioka, photographed here before his left hand was shot off by a B-29 tail gunner. Morioka's wingman during the unit's final wartime sortie on 15 August 1945 was Ens Mitsuo Tsurata, and he is standing in the second row, third from the right. (via Henry Sakaida)

flight was then ordered back to Atsugi, which was 'now under attack by Grummans'. There, he spotted six F6F-5s from VF-88 and shot one down.

The six inexperienced Hellcat pilots – Lt Howard Harrison, Lt(jg)s Maury Proctor, T. W. Hansen, Joseph Shaloff and Ens Wright Hobbs and Eugene Mandeberg – claimed that they were bounced by 'Franks' and 'Jacks' (the former being the JAAF's Nakajima Ki-84 and the 'Jack' the IJNAF Raiden). They claimed eight Japanese aircraft shot down for the loss of four of their own (Harrison, Shaloff, Hobbs and Mandeberg).

As the 14 Fleet Air Arm aircraft climbed through low cloud, they finally reached better weather at 6,000–8,000ft. The Seafire pilots were greeted by the new day's summer sun, and all was quiet except for the steady throb of their trusty Merlin engines. As the tiny strike force was crossing Tokyo Bay, a pair of A6M5 Zero-sens was sighted well below the Avengers. This was a common decoy tactic used by the Japanese, but the Seafire pilots did not bite. However, things became a little more interesting a few minutes later when a gaggle of a dozen A6M5s was seen coming down from the 'three o'clock-high' position. The R/Ts quickly crackled into life with the calls of 'Bogies – three o'clock-high'.

The diving Zero-sens passed the top cover and headed for the Avengers, as well as the close-escort Seafires below them. Sufficient warning was given for the pilots to counter the bounce, but not all were able to jettison their drop tanks. R/T failure doomed Sub Lt Freddie Hockley, and he was shot down in the first pass. He was the last Royal Navy casualty of the war.

In his memoirs, Lt Saburo Abe of the 252nd AG claims to have shot down a Seafire on 15 August, but his description does not match what happened to Seafire pilot Sub-Lt Hockley;

Immediately, it turned into a chaotic battle. Both the enemy fighters and ours were coming and going from all directions. I did not know how to determine my target. Suddenly, an enemy aeroplane appeared from my right and flew down to the left. At that moment, I remembered what Tetsuzo Iwamoto, a pilot officer, had taught me. Quickly, I banked to the left with full-throttle and chased the enemy fighter.

On the ground, I was pretty good at shooting. However, it was not the same when I had to shoot while flying a fighter aeroplane. I always missed my targets. So, I had decided that I would not pull the trigger lever until I was close enough to see an expression on my opponent's face. On that day, I did the same.

The enemy pilot probably felt my presence, and he looked back. Our eyes met for a moment. I saw his despairing look, and I opened fire at the same time. I did not need to use a gunsight. If I remember well, the distance between us was less than 20 metres. I pulled the trigger lever, and the next moment I saw that half of the pilot's head had been blown off. The windscreen of his aeroplane went red, being covered with blood. His fighter was tossed upward into the air as if it was bending its back. I flew under him and just managed to avoid a crash.

Lt Saburo Abe also claims to have been shot at by Seafires a few minutes later, causing him to force-land his fighter:

YUTAKA MORIOKA

By August 1945, there were three kinds of Japanese fighter pilot – the surviving experts, most of whom had joined Capt Minoru Genda's elite squadron (343rd Kokutai), armed with the very effective N1K2-J Shiden Kai ('George') fighter, the novices straight out of flight school and those assigned to the kamikaze units. But in August 1945, Lt Yutaka Morioka did not fit into any of these groups. He was one of the few who actually gained in experience in the last few months of the war and survived. Hours before the final surrender announcement on 15 August 1945, Lt Morioka would achieve ace status with his fifth, and final, victory. He was probably the last pilot to do so in World War II.

Born on 8 March 1922 to parents who worked in firearms and explosives distribution, Yutaka Morioka was a fearless leader and late starter in the fighter game. Entering the Naval Academy at Etajima in the 70th Class, he graduated on 11 November 1941 and began his training as a D3A 'Val' dive-bomber pilot. Morioka did not see any combat in the dive-bomber role, however, and instead became an instructor with the Usa Air Group in northern Kyushu.

With the war situation turning critical, Morioka, like hundreds of other pilots, was retrained to fly fighters. In April 1944 he joined the Atsugi-based 302nd Kokutai, whose job it was to shoot down B-29s heading for Tokyo and surrounding areas. The conversion for many pilots was not easy, but with the help of 27-kill Ens Sadaaki Akamatsu (the unit's ranking fighter ace), Morioka would be taught the finer points of aerial combat. In their first mock dogfighting session, Akamastu 'shot down' Morioka four times in just ten minutes. After two months of intensive training, Morioka was presented with a diploma.

Critical manpower shortages led Lt Morioka to become the youngest IJNAF squadron leader at the age of 23. Incredibly, he was given command of three squadrons, two equipped with Raidens and one with Zero-sens – Morioka preferred to fly the latter. On 23 January 1945 Morioka would lose his left hand when attacking a B-29 near Nagoya. The tail gunner managed to damage his Zero-sen and one of the 0.50-cal bullets severed Morioka's left hand. After a short stay in hospital, Morioka returned to his unit with an iron claw fitted in place of his missing hand.

(Via Henry Sakaida)

His fourth victory occurred on 3 August, when Morioka led four Zero-sens in an attempt to thwart the rescue of P-51 pilot Capt Edward Mikes Jr of the 458th FS, who had baled out over Tokyo Bay. Four Mustangs, two PB4Y-2 Privateers, a B-17, a B-29 and a submarine were all involved in the operation, and Morioka managed to shoot down a P-51 from the 457th FS. He and his comrades also strafed Capt Mikes in his lifeboat (which had been dropped by a B-17G from the 4th Emergency Rescue Squadron). Mikes survived with only a few scratches, and was later rescued.

Lt Morioka led another attack on a rescue mission ten days later when he and his pilots spotted a PBY that was trying to pick up a Hellcat pilot. Morioka and his formation of eight Zero-sens chased after the Catalina, which had managed to take-off and was heading for open water across Tokyo Bay at wave-top height. The PBY was eventually brought down by the IJNAF fighters at the very mouth of Tokyo Bay.

Becoming a certified practising accountant post-war, Morioka eventually passed away in July 1993.

I heard a loud noise and felt pain in my right leg as if someone had hit it with an iron bar. I felt like I was awakened from my trance or something. Still, I was thinking 'Idiot! Who are those stupid ones that cannot tell their friends from the enemy? I'm going to punch them when they get out of their aeroplanes', still thinking that I was being shot at by Japanese fighters. I looked up, and the two fighters that had shot at me passed above my Zero-sen and flew off to the left. 'There was no "rising sun" painted on them', I said to myself. They were not the American fighters. Their marking was different. 'Who is that? They're British. What are they doing here?'

Despite Lt Abe claiming to have inflicted a grievous head wound on Sub Lt Hockley, the later managed to bale out of his stricken Seafire prior to it hitting the water. He was later captured and executed by his captors.

The remaining Seafires turned into the Japanese fighters. With the first element of Zero-sens now out of range, Sub Lt Lowden moved his flight into line abreast and engaged the second group of aircraft. The first Zero-sen was shot down at long range by Sub Lt Lowden. Opening fire at 800 yards and ceasing at 450, he hit the Zero-sen hard, causing its undercarriage oleos to drop. Lowden's No 3, Sub Lt 'Taffy' Williams, also scored some hits, and was credited with a shared victory. With his port cannon now jammed, Sub Lt Lowden continued to strike a second Zero-sen from a distance of 250 yards – after three short bursts it blew up.

The opening moves had proved decisive for the Seafire pilots, with Lowden having shot down two Zero-sens, shared in the destruction of a third and damaged two more. Williams shot down an A6M on his own and also shared one with Lowden. Now it was Sub Lt Gerry 'Spud' Murphy's turn:

The enemy approached our Avengers in fairly close starboard echelon, but with flights in line astern. They peeled off smartly in fours from down sun and headed for the Avengers. One section of four appeared to be coming head-on for us, but I didn't observe their guns firing. Their original attack was well coordinated, but they seemed to lose each other after that, and could not have kept a good lookout astern.

I opened fire with my flight leader from the enemy's port quarter and saw strikes on the fuselage of the enemy, which was finished off by my flight leader or No 3. I disengaged from above to attack another 'Zeke' to port and 500ft below. Closed from above and astern, obtaining hits on its belly and engine, but I was closing too fast and overshot. I pulled up my nose to re-attack the No 2 and saw a lone 'Zeke' at my level doing a shallow turn to starboard. He evidently didn't see me, and I held my fire till 100 yards away. I observed immediate strikes on the cockpit and engine, which burst into flames. The enemy fighter rolled onto its back and plummeted in flames into cloud.

The close escort, tied as they were to the Avengers, still managed an impressive score. Sub Lt Don Duncan RNVR chose to retain his slipper tank, and keeping his speed up (as recommended in Naval Air Tactic Notes), he engaged three of the Zero-sens and came away with two probables to his name. The last Seafire to leave the combat area was flown by Duncan's section leader, Sub Lt Randy Kay. As an A6M

This detailed close up shows the wing-mounted armament of the late model A6M5c. This variant was the most heavily-armed and best protected of the Zero-sen family, having an armoured glass windscreen, self-sealing fuel tanks and pilot head armour. Within each wing was a 20mm cannon, and outboard of the cannon was a 13mm machine gun. A further heavy machine gun was installed above the engine on the starboard side. The A6M5c was equipped with the Nakajima Sakae Model 31A engine, which boasted water-methanol injection. (Aeroplane Monthly)

closed on the Avengers, he made a quarter attack that set the enemy fighter's port wing root area on fire. Switching targets, he then concentrated on another Zero-sen, and with a high deflection shot blew its tail off with his first burst. Searching for a third target Kay found, and damaged, another A6M5c.

All six of the Avengers delivered their bombs on target. Only one had been badly damaged by the surprise Zero-sen attack, and its pilot nursed the crippled aircraft back to the fleet and ditched alongside one of the radar picket destroyers.

Returning to *Indefatigable* on his own, Sub Lt Lowden encountered a dozen Corsairs (probably from VBF-88). They had seen the combat from a distance and were eager to make a contribution. By lowering his wheels and flaps and turning tightly to show his markings, Lowden was able to convince his potentially trigger happy Allies that he was a 'friendly'.

302nd Kokutai records for 15 August indicate that a mixed formation of 12+ interceptors engaged enemy carrier aircraft in the Tokyo area and claimed a single kill and two probables for the loss of four fighters. These statistics closely match British records, as Seafires from the 24th Naval Fighter Wing claimed to have engaged 12 Zero-sens and shot seven of them down. Three more were claimed as probables and four damaged. The 252nd Kokutai was credited with downing nine enemy aircraft and damaging four more that day. Finally, VF-88 claimed eight enemy aircraft destroyed for the loss of four of its own.

The stress and confusion of aerial combat routinely caused inflated and overoptimistic claims to be made on both sides, and the events of that day were most certainly clouded by the 'fog of war'. Which Japanese unit actually

Some of the Fleet Air Arm's best. These pilots were involved in the Royal Navy's last air combat of the war. They are, from left to right, Sub Lts Don Duncan, Randy Kay, 'Spud' Murphy, Vic Lowden, Ted Gavin and 'Taffy' Williams, all from No 24 Naval Fighter Wing embarked in *Indefatigable*. They were credited with seven Zero-sens shot down on 15 August 1945. (via Andrew Thomas)

One of the hardest shots to make in aerial combat was the deflection shot. The majority of fighter pilots found it extremely difficult, and only the best mastered the art. In order to shoot at a target with high deflection, the pilot first had to position his fighter in the right part of the sky. Next, he had to aim at a point in space somewhere in front of his intended victim. This required the pilot to quickly calculate distance, angle, approach speed, convergences, line of target flight and deflection, and then fly and shoot at the same time. If everything went as planned, his bullets and the intended victim would meet at the same time.

The new GGS Mk 2 gyro gunsight fitted to most Seafires in 1945 was created in an attempt to solve the problems associated with deflection shooting. However, in a twisting, turning, dogfight the sight was seldom on target for more than a few seconds, and the tracking was not very smooth. The GGS Mk 2 proved to be far more adept when used against a target that was steadily approached from astern. It did have a 'fixed cross' aiming point for dogfighting manoeuvres, although this gave the pilot less aiming information than the old GM2 gunsight that the GGS Mk 2 had replaced!

found and attacked the Fleet Air Arm Avengers and Seafires remains a mystery. It is quite possible that elements from both the 302nd and 252nd Kokutais were involved. What is for certain is the fact that these engagements over Tokyo Bay were the very last dogfights to be fought in World War II. Which group of fighters actually participated in the final air combat of the conflict remains unknown to this day.

These A6M5c Type 52cs of the 252nd Kokutai warm up their engines prior to flying another home air defence mission in the summer of 1945. In the hands of a highly skilled pilot the Zero-sen was still a formidable opponent even at this late stage of the war. Its heavy armament of three 13.2mm machine guns and two 20mm cannons gave it a heavy punch, and one that was equal to, and in some cases better than, the best Allied fighters in-theatre. (via Henry Sakaida)

Clear skies and calm seas. Seafire IIIs of No 24 Naval Fighter Wing ready for take-off during peacetime flight operations somewhere off New Zealand. This shot was taken in November 1945, just prior to the wing disembarking for a two-week stay ashore. *Indefatigable* and its Seafires left the British Pacific Fleet at the end of January 1946. (Fleet Air Arm Museum)

STATISTICS AND ANALYSIS

In terms of numbers of aircraft shot down, the Seafire's contribution during World War II was negligible at best. The Fleet Air Arm was credited with 455.5 aerial victories in six years of war, and American-built fighters contributed more than a third of these –52 for the F6F Hellcat, 52.5 for the F4U Corsair and 67 for the F4F Wildcat. Seafire pilots claimed 37 kills, 15 of which were Zero-sens. The remaining 247 aircraft were credited to the Sea Hurricanes, Fireflies, Fulmars, Sea Gladiators and Skuas.

As detailed in the previous chapter, the Seafire's last aerial combat of the war proved to be a resounding success. Starved of action since 9 May 1945, the young pilots of No 24 Naval Fighter Wing had shown the aircraft to be an excellent fighter. The efforts of wing leaders, squadron COs, pilots and maintenance personnel in the Pacific had effectively extinguished the Seafire's poor reputation. When operated by motivated and well-trained personnel, the fighter was able to achieve some remarkable results.

In eight days of action between 17 July and 15 August 1945, 2,331 combat sorties were flown off the four British carriers in-theatre. Some 1,186 of those were by the 88 Seafires of Nos 24 and 38 Naval Fighter Wings. That is 51 percent of the sorties flown by 35 percent of the aircraft embarked!

When fitted with 89- and 90-gallon drop tanks, the Seafires were able to achieve some outstanding offensive numbers. With a radius of action in the 200-mile range, they contributed 324 sorties against airfields and flew 157 anti-shipping strikes. These sorties saw 43,600 rounds of 20mm cannon and 169,270 rounds of 0.303-in machine gun ammunition expended. The damage dished out was extensive – 87 aircraft destroyed on the ground, 3,700 tons of shipping sunk and 24,700 tons damaged.

In return, Seafire losses were slight. Just eight aircraft were lost to flak and one to enemy fighters, with six pilots killed in action – a loss rate of 1.9 percent, which was lower than the 2.4 percent figure for Fleet Air Arm squadrons within Task Force 37. Twenty Seafires were also written off aboard the two carriers, seven of which were damaged beyond local repair and seven lost operationally.

What the Seafire achieved in the last few months of the Pacific War had more to do with the personnel who flew and maintained it rather than the aircraft itself. While it was a poor carrier fighter (arguably, there were only two ideal carrier fighters built during World War II, the Hellcat and Zero-sen), in terms of its poor range and ruggedness for deck operations, the Seafire's combat ability as a fighter at the end of the war was still second to none.

The Spitfire's contribution to Allied victory was immense. The 'stretch' in the Spitfire's design allowed it to add more horsepower and armament without degrading its performance. The Griffon-powered Mk XIV (the last version to see widespread service during the war) was considered by many to be the best piston-engined fighter of the conflict.

The IJNAF's reluctance to add more horsepower to the Zero-sen doomed the fighter well before the appearance of the Seafire. Indeed, it was not until November 1944 that Mitsubishi was finally given the go ahead to install its Kinsei 62 engine, rated at 1,350hp (still 235hp less than the Merlin 55M). Only two prototypes were ever built.

The inability of the Japanese to produce better versions of the Zero-sen, or to introduce a replacement, meant its fighter pilots were forced to fly the A6M until the very end of the war. Japanese industry also underperformed throughout the war. Between January and July 1945, Mitsubishi and Nakajima were able to produce only 1,578 Zero-sens.

In the end, the Zero-sen was both an example of Japanese genius and hardheadedness. Ironically, the last three months of air combat in the Pacific actually saved the lives of hundreds of young IJNAF airmen. The hoarding of aircraft and fuel for

The A6M5c was the primary opponent of the Seafire in the final months of World War II, and virtually all aerial claims made by Fleet Air Arm fighter pilots in 1945 were against this aircraft.
(Aeroplane Monthly)

one last kamikaze effort had the opposite effect. The final battle never came, and the thousands of pilots trained for imperial service were spared.

The Seafire's shortcomings were many and varied, but it was more than fitting that on the last day of the war Reginald Mitchell's elegant elliptical-winged fighter took part in what might have been the last dogfight of World War II.

Seafire vs A6M Zero-Sen Confirmed Kills					
Pilot	**Unit**	**Date**	**Aircraft Serial**	**Kill(s)**	**Aircraft Carrier**
Sub Lt R. H. Reynolds	894 NAS	1/4/45	Seafire L III PR256/S 146	2 x A6Ms	*Indefatigable*
Sub Lt J. H. Kernahan	887 NAS	12/4/45	Seafire L III ?????/S 137	A6M	*Indefatigable*
CPO I. B. Bird	887 NAS	4/5/45	Seafire L III NN363/S ???	A6M	*Indefatigable*
Sub Lt D. T. Challick	887 NAS	4/5/45	Seafire L III ?????/S 131	A6M	*Indefatigable*
Sub Lt C. S. Randal	894 NAS	4/5/45	Seafire L III NF521/S 130	0.5 A6M	*Indefatigable*
Lt A. S. Macleod	894 NAS	4/5/45	Seafire L III PR254/S 145	A6M	*Indefatigable*
Sub Lt R. H. Reynolds	894 NAS	4/5/45	Seafire L III ?????/S 141	0.5 A6M	*Indefatigable*
Sub Lt A. W. Bradley	894 NAS	8/5/45	Seafire L III NN284/S 153	0.25 A6M	*Indefatigable*
Sub Lt K. D. Gall	894 NAS	8/5/45	Seafire L III ?????/S 136	0.25 A6M	*Indefatigable*
Sub Lt F. S. Hockley	894 NAS	8/5/45	Seafire L III ?????/S 143	0.25 A6M	*Indefatigable*
Sub Lt J. C. Taylor	894 NAS	8/5/45	Seafire L III ?????/S 137	0.25 A6M	*Indefatigable*
Sub Lt V. S. Lowden	887 NAS	15/8/45	Seafire L III LR866/S 121	2 x A6Ms	*Indefatigable*
Sub Lt V. S. Lowden	887 NAS	15/8/45	Seafire L III LR866/S 121	0.5 A6M	*Indefatigable*
Sub Lt C. S. Randal	894 NAS	15/8/45	Seafire L III NN584/S ???	A6M	*Indefatigable*
Sub Lt G. J. Murphy	887 NAS	15/8/45	Seafire L III NN212/S 112	2 x A6Ms	*Indefatigable*
Sub Lt W. J. Williams	887 NAS	15/8/45	Seafire L III ?????/S ???	A6M	*Indefatigable*
Sub Lt W. J. Williams	887 NAS	15/8/45	Seafire L III ?????/S ???	0.5 A6M	*Indefatigable*

AFTERMATH

The war in the Pacific was now over. Royal Navy strength was quickly reduced in the Far East. By mid September 1945, the only operational carriers in-theatre were *Indefatigable*, *Implacable* and three new Light Fleet carriers. No 24 Naval Fighter Wing was finally disbanded on 15 March 1946, while No 38 Naval Fighter Wing was re-designated as 801 NAS after absorbing 880 NAS on 13 September 1945. It would later be equipped with 18 Seafire IIIs and, eventually, 18 new Seafire XVs.

Because the latter were not cleared for decking landing, 801 NAS continued to operate Mk IIIs, and it was the last frontline unit in Royal Navy service to be equipped with the type. The squadron disbanded on 3 June 1946. Many L Mk IIIs were used by fighter training squadrons, and they served for two more years until replaced by later marks. A total of 1,163 Seafire IIIs were built.

Four other air forces were issued with surplus Seafires post-war. Canada was the only Commonwealth country to choose the aircraft for its navy, and it formed two squadrons with Seafire L IIIs – these were later replaced by Mk XVs between June and September 1945. The French Navy's *Aeronavale* was also equipped with no fewer than 113 L IIIs between March 1946 and June 1948 – a further 15 Griffon-powered Seafire 15s were acquired in June 1949. The French used their Seafires in operations against communist Viet Minh insurgents in Indochina in November 1949. Burma obtained 20 Seafire 15s in 1951 for operations against several groups, including Chinese Nationalists, Burmese separatists and communists. Finally, the Irish Air Corps received a dozen de-navalised L Mk IIIs in 1947.

For all of its faults, the Seafire continued to be produced, and used, by the Royal Navy. The last version to see service, and the last to see combat, was the FR Mk 47. This was the ultimate stage in the development of the Griffon-engined Seafire line (comprised of the Mks XV, 17, 45, 46 and 47). The FR Mk 47 did not look like the

aircraft conceived by R. J Mitchell 14 years earlier. It was a streamlined, but muscle-bound, fighter with a massive fin and rudder. The armament was increased to four 20mm cannon. The Griffon 88 engine gave combat outputs of 2,350hp at 1,250ft and 2,145hp at 15,500ft. A six-bladed contra-rotating propeller was required to absorb all of this raw power, and the landing gear was strengthened and widened in track by a foot.

The Mk 47 version of the Seafire would experience combat operations following the 25 June 1950 invasion of South Korea by the North Korean People's Army. The carrier HMS *Triumph* was ordered to provide support for the retreating army of the Republic of Korea. Between 1 July and 20 September 1950, the 12 Seafires of 800 NAS flew 245 CAP and search sorties and 115 strike sorties for the loss of just two aircraft – one suffered an arrestor gear malfunction and subsequently ditched and the other Seafire was shot down in error by a nervous gunner in a USAF B-29.

The aircraft finally passed from frontline service in November 1950, although Royal Navy Volunteer Reserve unit 1833 NAS did not retire its last Seafire 47 until 1954. After a decade of fleet service, and nearly 10,000 combat sorties, the Seafire had done its part.

ZERO-SEN

At the time of the Japanese surrender, A6M5s of various sub-types served with only six frontline units (the 203rd, 252nd, 302nd, 352nd, 721st and Yokosuka Kokutais) on the home islands. With a few exceptions (several airframes were shipped to the United States for evaluation), all remaining Zero-sens were burned or destroyed where they stood. Others located on island bases and areas the Allies had by-passed were simply left to rot.

A grand total of 10,094 Zero-sens were built, along with a further 327 floatplane fighters and 517 two-seat trainers. Mitsubishi was responsible for 3,879 airframes and Nakajima produced 6,215 A6M1 to A6M8 fighters.

The 'pugnacious' J2M3 Raiden was to be one of the Zero-sen's wartime replacements. Poor production management and a long development period resulted in the fighter being unavailable until December 1943, however. The Raiden made its combat debut during the battle of the Marianas in September 1944. It was also heavily involved in the defence of the Japanese home islands. These Raidens belong to the 1st Hikotai of the 302nd Kokutai at Atsugi in 1945. (via Henry Sakaida)

The IJNAF did not plan for a long war, nor did it see the Zero-sen having a prolonged service life. As a consequence, there were no new fighters being planned or developed to replace the venerable A6M. Not until 20 March 1942 did the new Mitsubishi J2M1 Raiden, code named 'Jack' by the Allies, take flight. This aircraft was designed as an interceptor to destroy enemy bombers and out-perform enemy fighters. Armed with four 20mm cannon, the J2M3 Model 21 had a top speed of 371mph at 17,860ft. Poor production management limited the number of Raidens built to just 470, however.

The other IJNAF fighter to see mass production towards the end of the war was the Kawanishi N1K2 Shiden-Kai, code named 'George'. It was hoped that this aircraft would finally replace the Zero-sen, but only 1,400 examples of this outstanding fighter were ever built.

Today, there are a handful of Zero-sens flying, mostly in the United States, with approximately 13 others that can be found in museums around the world. There are presently no airworthy Merlin-engined Seafires.

Wherever British and American carrier task forces went, Zero-sens were destroyed in large numbers. Most of the Japanese atolls, islands and military installations targeted were bombed and shelled beyond recognition. This wrecked A6M5 on Kwajalein Atoll in February 1944 is a stark reminder of the growing force of the Allied war machine by this stage of the conflict. (WW2Colour.com)

FURTHER READING

BOOKS

Bergerud, E. M., *Fire In the Sky* (Westview Press, 2001)

Bodie, W. M. and Ethell, J., *World War II Pacific War Eagles in Original Colour* (Widewing Publications, 1997)

Brown, D., *The British Pacific and East Indies Fleets – 'The Forgotten Fleets' 50th Anniversary'* (Brodie Publishing Ltd, 1995)

Brown, D., *The Seafire* (Ian Allen, 1973)

Caidin, M., *Zero Fighter* (Ballantine Books Inc, 1971)

Crosley, Cdr R. M., *They Gave Me a Seafire* (Airlife, 2001)

Donald, D. and March, D. J., *Carrier Aviation Air Power Directory* (AIRtime Publishing, 2001)

Ethell, J. L. et al., *Great Book of World War II Airplanes* (Bonanza Books, 1984)

Francillon, R. J., *Japanese Aircraft of the Pacific War* (Naval Institute Press, 1994)

Freeman, J. and Robinson, N., *On Target Profile 5 - Supermarine Seafire Mk Ib – Mk 47* (The Aviation Workshop, 2004)

Green, W., *Fighters Volume Three* (Macdonald & Co Ltd, 1961)

Hata, I. and Yasuho, I., *Japanese Naval Aces and Fighter Units in World War II* (Naval Institute Press, 1989)

Hata, K., *August 15th Sky* (Bungeishunju-sha Publishing)

Hooton, T. and Ward, R., *Aircam Aviation Series No 8, Supermarine Spitfire Mk XII-24 Supermarine Seafire Mk I-47* (Osprey Publishing, 1969)

Jarrett, P., *Aircraft of the Second World War* (Putnam 1997)

Mikesh, R. C., *Broken Wing of the Samurai: The Destruction of the Japanese Air Force* (Airlife, 1993)

Nijboer, D., *Cockpit: An Illustrated History* (Boston Mills Press, 1998)

Nijboer, D., *Graphic War – The Secret Aviation Drawings and Illustrations of World War II* (Boston Mills Press, 2005)

Nohara, S., *A6M Zero in Action* (Squadron/Signal Publications, 1983)

Okumiya, M. Horikoshi, and Caidin, M., *Zero* (Ballantine Books, 1973)

Price, A., *Fighter Aircraft* (Arms and Armour Press, 1989)

Price, A., *Spitfire at War* (Ian Allan Ltd, 1974)

Sakai, S., *Samurai* (Ballantine Books, 1963)

Sakaida, H., *Osprey Aircraft of the Aces 22 – Imperial Japanese Navy Aces 1937–45* (Osprey Publishing, 1998)

Smith, D. S. and Richards, M. C., *Profile 236 Mitsubishi A6M5 to A6M8* (Profile Publications Ltd, 1967)

Smith, P. C., *Task Force 57: The British Pacific Fleet 1944–45 (*William Kimber & Company Ltd, 1969)

Shacklady, E. and Morgan, E. B., *Spitfire – The History* (Key Books Ltd, 2000)

Sturtivant, R., and Balance, T., *The Squadrons of the Fleet Air Arm* (Air Britain, 1994)

Styling, M., *Aircraft of the Aces 8 – Corsair Aces of World War 2* (Osprey Publishing, 1995)

Thomas, A., *Aircraft of the Aces 75 – Royal Navy Aces of World War 2* (Osprey Publishing, 2007)

Tillman, B., *Osprey Aircraft of the Aces 10 – Hellcat Aces of World War 2* (Osprey Publishing, 1996)

Tillman, B., *US Navy Fighter Squadrons in World War II* (Specialty Press, 1997)

Wragg, D., *Fleet Air Arm Handbook* (Sutton Publishing Ltd, 2003)

The Japanese Air Forces in World War II (Arms and Armour Press, 1979)

MAGAZINE ARTICLES

Brown, E. Capt., 'Spitfires with Sea Legs Parts 1 & 2', *Air International* (September and October 1978)

Francillon, R., 'Zero - Japan's Greatest Fighter', *Air International* (January 1992)

Huggins, M., 'The Final Combat', *Aeroplane Monthly* (June 2001)

Meyer, C., '1944 Fighter Conference', *Flight Journal Special WWII Fighters* (February 2001)

Morioka, Lt. Y., 'The Last Day of the Atsugi Kokutai', *Maru* (1973)

Saburo, A., 'I Shot Down a Spitfire', *Maru Extra* No 24 (September 2000)

Sakaida, H., 'The Last Dogfight of WW II', *Foundation Magazine* (1985)

WEBSITES

www.combinedfleet.com

www.navweapons.com

www.spitfireperformance.com

www.j-aircraft.com

www.fleetairarmarchive.net

INDEX